Sales Management:
Products and Services

Sales Management
Products and Services

Dr Jae K Shim MBA, PHD

Professor of Business
California State University, Long Beach
and
CEO
Delta Consulting Company

Global Professional Publishing
Random Acres
Slip Mill Lane
Hawkhurst
Cranbrook
Kent TN18 5AD
Email: publishing@gppbooks.com
Website: www.gppbooks.com

ISBN 978-1-906403-79-9

Printed in the United Kingdom by 4edge Ltd

Contents

CONTENTS

Preface

Sales Management is concerned with all activities, processes and decisions involved in managing the sales function in an organization. It involves planning the selling program and implementing and controlling the personal selling effort of the firm. Sales management in the twenty-first century is characterized by

- Innovation fuels success in selling today.
- Sales effectiveness is enhanced through technology. Sales management must be smart and nimble and provide technology-centered solutions to support the sales effort.
- Leadership is a key component in sales management success.
- Sales management is a global endeavor.
- Ethics underlies all selling and sales management activities.
- Social media marketing comes of age.

This book is an overview of the role of the sales manager, both at headquarters and in the field, in managing salespeople, personal selling, IT resources, and functions of marketing. The problems of organizing, forecasting, planning, communicating, evaluating, and controlling sales are analyzed. A variety of techniques and pertinent concepts of behavioral science are applied to the management of the sales effort and sales force. Key trends, such as online advertising and social media marketing, affecting sales organizations and sales managers today are highlighted

About the Author

Dr. Jae K. Shim is a professor of business at California State University, Long Beach and CEO of Delta Consulting Company, a management consulting and training firm. Dr. Shim received his M.B.A. and Ph.D. degrees from the University of California at Berkeley (Haas School of Business). Dr. Shim has been a consultant to commercial and nonprofit organizations for over 30 years.

Dr. Shim has over 50 college and professional books to his credit, including, *Budgeting Basics and Beyond, 2012-2013 Corporate Controller's Handbook of Financial Management, Dictionary of Business Terms, The Complete CPA Reference, CFO Fundamentals,* and the best-selling *Vest-Pocket MBA.*

Thirty-three of his publications have been translated into foreign languages such as Chinese, Spanish, Russian, Polish, Croatian, Italian, Japanese, Indonesian and Korean. Professor Shim's books have been published by CCH, Barron's, John Wiley, McGraw-Hill, Prentice-Hall, Penguins Portfolio, Thomson Reuters, Global Publishing, and American Management Association (Amacom).

Dr. Shim has also published numerous articles in professional and academic journals. He was the recipient of the Financial Management Association International's *1982 Credit Research Foundation Award* for his article on cash flow forecasting and financial modeling.

Dr. Shim has been frequently quoted by such media as the *Los Angeles Times, Orange County Register, Business Start-ups, Personal Finance, and Money Radio.* He also provides business content for CPE e-learning providers and for m-learning providers such as iPhone, iPad, iPod, Blackberry, Android, and Window Phones.

CHAPTER 1

Sales Management and Selling: Its Development and Role in American Society

Sales management is concerned with all activities, processes and decisions involved in managing the sales function in an organization. It involves planning the selling program and implementing and controlling the personal selling effort of the firm. Sales Management in the Twenty-First Century is characterized by

- Innovation fuels success in selling today.
- Sales effectiveness is enhanced through technology. Sales management must be smart and nimble and provide technology-centered solutions to support the sales effort.
- Leadership is a key component in sales management success.
- Sales management is a global endeavor.

▶ Ethics underlies all selling and sales management activities.

▶ Social media marketing comes of age.

The applications of personal selling

The Definitions Committee of the American Marketing Association defines selling as "the personal or impersonal process of assisting and/or persuading a prospective customer to buy a commodity or service or to act favorably upon an idea that has commercial significance to the seller." However, in actual practice, the applications of salesmanship are much broader in scope, for it is an activity which permeates almost every avenue of human endeavor. The ability to convince people is a necessary skill for lawyers, teachers, ministers, politicians, and many others. It is a skill used by the doctor when she attempts to convince her patient that she should stop smoking; or a skill used by a mother when she explains to her young son that stealing is wrong. Actually, then, personal selling is the ability to influence and convince others, and we practice it almost every day.

Scope and significance of personal selling and sales management

Personal selling is a useful vehicle for communicating with present and potential buyers.

Nature of Personal Selling and Sales Management

▶ **Personal selling** involves the two-way flow of communication between a buyer and seller, often in a face-to-face encounter, designed to influence a person's or group's purchase decision.

▶ Personal selling also occurs by telephone, through video teleconferencing, and the Internet between buyers and sellers.

▶ The tasks involved in managing personal selling include: (1) setting objectives; (2) organizing the sales force; (3) recruiting, selecting, training, and compensating salespeople; and (4) evaluating the performance of individual salespeople.

Personal Selling in Marketing

▶ Salespeople match company interests with customer needs to satisfy both parties in the exchange process.

▶ Salespeople represent what a company is or attempts to be and are often the only personal contact a customer has with the firm.

▶ Personal selling may play a dominant role in a firm's marketing program if a firm uses a push marketing strategy.

Creating Customer Value through Salespeople: Relationship and Partnership Selling

Salespeople can create customer value in many ways:

1. Identifying creative solutions to customer problems.
2. Easing the customer buying process.
3. Following through after the sale.

Relationship selling is the practice of building ties to customers based on a salesperson's attention and commitment to customer needs over time. It:

1. Involves mutual respect and trust among buyers and sellers.
2. Focuses on creating long-term customers, not one-time sales.

Partnership selling (or ***enterprise selling***) is the practice whereby buyers and sellers combine their expertise and resources to create customized solutions, commit to joint planning, and share customer, competitive, and company information for their mutual benefit, and ultimately the customer. It:

1. Relies on cross-functional business specialists who apply their knowledge and expertise to achieve higher productivity, lower cost, and greater customer value.
2. Complements supplier and channel partnering.

Relationship and partnership selling represent another dimension of customer relationship management (CRM).

The contributions of selling

Personal selling plays an important role in our lives. Among its functions in, and contributions to, our business and economic system are the following:

1. It has helped make the United States one of the most productive economies in the world.
2. It has given our country the highest standard of living in the world.
3. It is the major objective of every business enterprise and the only function that generates direct revenue and profits. In this sense, then, it is the heart of our business economy.

4. It helps to maintain the spirit of competition, which is the basis for a free enterprise system.
5. In today's mass society, "the world will not beat a path to your door," and selling becomes the bridge for introducing new products and services.
6. When a new product or service is introduced by a competitive firm, a company offering an established product or service will often rely on improved salesmanship to retain its share of the market.

New concepts in selling

Our economy has shifted from a "manufacturing-oriented" economy to a "marketing-oriented' economy. This means that we generally do not first design and manufacture a product and then decide how to market or sell it. Instead, we first carefully study the marketplace to determine what the consumer needs and wants. Selling and promotional strategies are also determined, and then the product is designed and manufactured in accordance with these factors. In applying this concept, the function of selling becomes more important in the total business environment and involves a greater degree of coordination with the other business functions.

Each year more and more companies are operating on the basis of this "marketing concept." Those who adopt this marking approach make important changes in their methods, usually with improved results. They focus on satisfying the consumer, but they also zero in on the accomplishment of the company's objectives - increased sales volume, larger share of the market, but above all, if the company is to survive, adequate profits. All aspects of the business are integrated to achieve these goals. No longer is production allowed to become an end in itself or to dominate company polices.

In short, the marketing concept envisions a total system of operation in which satisfying the consumer leads to profitable sales. Satisfying the consumer is the means of achieving long-run as well as immediate profits. The customer, then, becomes the pivot supporting all the activities of the business. Implementation of this philosophy requires teamwork by all those in marketing research, product planning, sales forecasting, advertising, selling, physical distribution, sales analysis and control, and other related marketing activities. Selling plays a key role in this combined effort because a customer is not satisfied nor is a profit made until the product or service is actually sold.

Business today is also influenced by more competition, both domestically and from abroad. There are more rigid cost controls, and more and better information is now available regarding the products and services we buy—particularly over the Internet. Furthermore, labor, material, and operating costs have greatly increased, and profit margins are therefore narrower. All of these conditions have made the work of the salesperson more important and complex. Accordingly, selling today requires more knowledge and skill.

The modern salesperson must not only be skillful in selling her product or service but must also be able to show the individual customer how to use the product or service in solving her particular needs or problems. If she sells a product to a merchant, she may also be required to show the merchant how to retail the product and be prepared to advise her on activities ranging from choosing a store location to developing inventory methods, preparing advertising, analyzing consumer behavior, setting prices, and others. With this expansion in the activities of selling, the modern salesperson of today must be knowledgeable in many areas of business and be capable of adjusting to a multitude of varying circumstances.

Is salesmanship an art or a science?

To qualify as a science in the strictest sense, salesmanship would have to make greater use than it does of the "scientific method." This method proceeds in definite stages: first, data is gathered through observation; second, hypotheses are formulated through inductive reasoning; and third, the hypotheses are tested through further observation and controlled experiment. In science, the several variables involved in the experiment can be controlled, and the experiment will always produce the same result under the same conditions no matter when, where or by whom performed. For example, chemistry is a science in this sense because all the variables such as compounds, weight, and temperatures can be controlled with exact preciseness. Consequently, an experiment can be conducted today, tomorrow, next year, or even a hundred years from now and the same results can be obtained.

However, in selling, the several variables affecting the sale, such as customer behavior, competitive activity, the weather, and general economic conditions, cannot be controlled. Furthermore, each customer is different from all others in some way. Hence, each sales situation is uniquely different, and the salesperson's approach must be varied according to the specific circumstance that prevails in each case. For these reasons, selling is not a science and will remain an art as long as there are varying circumstances and individual differences. But, this does not mean that the salesperson can be careless and lackadaisical in her approach to selling. On the contrary, the varied and ever-changing circumstances make it all the more necessary for her to be alert and well organized.

Must you be a born salesperson or can salesmanship be taught and learned?

Some people still believe that in order to be a success in selling one must have a magnetic personality, a silver tongue, and a firm handshake. It is true that a person who possesses these qualities will certainly have the edge over one who does not. However, to say that you must be born with a certain set of traits to succeed in selling is as ridiculous as saying that you are born a lawyer, a doctor, or a minister. All of these professions had to be mastered through years of study and training. Salesmanship can also be mastered. But to be successful with it, you must be able to discipline yourself and constantly strive to improve your performance.

 ## Indicate whether each of the following statements is true or false

1. If you build a better mousetrap, the world will beat a path to your door.
2. The United States has shifted from a "manufacturing-oriented" economy to a "marketing-oriented" economy.
3. Through careful analysis of the market and years of practice, salesmanship has become a science in the strict sense of the word.
4. People who lack the natural skills of a born salesperson may learn these skills by studying and practicing.

Answer

1. False. In today's mass society, the makers and users of new products and services are widely separated, and selling is the bridge that brings buyers and sellers together.
2. True. Today in the United States, firms first determine consumer wants and needs and then they produce what is desired. Further, selling must be coordinated with other business functions to solve customer needs.
3. False. Selling is an art, because each sales situation is uniquely different and the salesperson's approach must vary according to the circumstances.
4. True. Salesmanship can be learned, but one must discipline oneself to study and practice so that one may improve her performance.

CHAPTER 2

The Salesperson's Responsibilities and Qualifications

Successful selling does not end with getting the initial order; it builds volume by generating repeat orders that continue as long as the customer has a need for the product or service the salesperson is selling. From this standpoint, the major objective of selling is to serve and satisfy the buyer. Outwitting the customer and putting something over on her for the sake of earning a commission is detrimental not only to the buyer but also to the salesperson and her company as well. Such a sale creates a dissatisfied buyer; and if she is dissatisfied, there will be no repeat business. Selling today, therefore, emphasizes an approach, which is genuinely "buyer oriented" and it begins and continues by fulfilling the customer's particular needs and wants.

Her responsibility to the company

The salesperson also has important responsibilities to her company. In many cases, she is the only contact the buyer has with the company, and, therefore, becomes responsible for projecting the corporate image. She is also responsible for selling the product or service at a profit for the company. If she sells a product which pleases the buyer and earns her a commission but does not result in a profit for the company, she will not be a successful salesperson. A company must make a profit if it is to continue in business.

In addition to her selling duties, a salesperson is responsible for filling out orders, completing reports, collecting market information in the field, and following through on customer service and complaints. Her responsibilities to the company then are fourfold:

a) She must do everything she can do to project a favorable image.
b) She must sell in such a manner as to produce reasonable profits for her company.
c) She must provide the company with reports and other related information.
d) She must follow through on customer service and complaints.

Qualifications for selling

The qualifications necessary for successful selling will vary with the type of product or service being sold. For example, the salesperson who sells industrial equipment must know a great deal about designing, mechanical engineering, and current research in the field. On the other hand, the product knowledge and degree of preparation is less complex for the counter saleslady who sells handkerchiefs. Furthermore, although much has been written on this subject, no two companies will completely agree on the ranking of desirable traits necessary for successful selling. Nonetheless, the traits or characteristics discussed in the remainder of this chapter frequently are listed and certainly will help a person to be more effective salesperson.

? Indicate whether each of the following statements is true or false

1. The primary concern of a salesperson is to get the initial order by "putting over a deal."
2. Salespeople should only be concerned with selling products which please customers and not be concerned with corporate profits.
3. Salespeople have other duties to the company besides selling goods and services at a profit.
4. There are certain traits or characteristics that will help any salesperson to be more effective.

Answer

1. False. Successful selling means getting the initial order and continuing repeat sales by being "buyer oriented" and creating satisfied buyers.
2. False. Salespeople are responsible for selling products and services at a profit for the company; or else the company might go out of business.

3. True. In addition to their sales duties, salespeople must project a favorable image for the firm, provide reports and other information, and follow through on customer service and complaints.

4. True. Although no two companies agree on the ranking of desirable traits for salespeople, there are some traits or characteristics that are discussed most frequently as being helpful.

Product knowledge

The first requirement for successful selling is product knowledge. The salesperson is responsible for explaining the benefits and uses of her product or service, showing how it fulfills or solves the prospect's needs or problems, and answering the prospect's questions and objections. If she is poorly prepared or inadequately informed about her product, she will do a poor job in meeting these responsibilities. It will also impair her ability to gain the prospect's respect and confidence. Hence, successful selling begins with product knowledge. The salesperson needs to know something about the history and organization of the company; how the product is made; its benefits and uses; how it compares with competitor products; and how to operate, maintain, or care for it. She should be well informed as to prices: different sizes, styles, or models; payment methods; shipping or delivery procedures; guarantees and warranties; and service and adjustment polices.

Positive attitude

Selling is not an occupation that is completely devoid of tension, frustration, and insecurity. On top of this, a sufficient number of social and economic problems plague our society to drive almost anyone to the brink of despair. However, if we approach our problems with a negative or defeatist attitude, we generally are licked at the start. Our attitude determines our behavior; and our behavior, in turn, will determine our performance. In practice, "a positive attitude" means to minimize worry about problems and to concentrate on ways and means to solve them. It means to be optimistic rather than pessimistic. If the salesperson is to make the prospect positive minded about her product or service, she herself must possess and manifest this feeling.

Enthusiasm

Enthusiasm is the strong desire and interest a person feels when he believes that what he is doing or experiencing is exciting and worthwhile. It is a feeling of strongly liking something and being fervently absorbed in it. A salesperson who sells with enthusiasm is alive and dynamic. It is vital for her to feel this way; for if she has little enthusiasm for her product, it is extremely difficult, if not impossible, for her to convince the buyer of its merits. Enthusiasm is comparable to the fuel which fires the machine. It is a necessary trait for effective and successful selling, and as Lincoln once said, "Nothing great was ever accomplished without enthusiasm."

Confidence

Confidence is a belief that you can achieve what you wish to accomplish. It is self-assurance, reliance, and faith. If you want to do something but believe you can't, the chances that you will fail are much greater than if you approach your task with a determination to succeed. In order to develop confidence in the buyer, the salesperson must first have confidence in herself. Inevitably, the environment in which selling is done will challenge the salesperson, and if she lacks confidence in herself or her product, she will generally be unsuccessful.

Liking people

A salesperson has to like people, because products and services are sold through and to people, and liking people means much more than just being friendly. For the salesperson it means continuing to like people even when she believes they are wrong or when they make her discouraged or angry. Liking people also means trying to understand them, and doing everything you possibly can to help them.

Empathy

Empathy is "putting yourself in the other fellow's shoes." It means a sensitivity to the feelings and interest of others. Empathy also involves skill in analyzing how others are reacting to what you are saying and doing. A strong sense of empathy is an important quality for successful selling; and a salesperson who lacks it is at a serious disadvantage in attempting to convince the prospect on the merits of her product or service.

Ability to communicate and persuade

The ability to communicate involves four phases:
   a) Getting the person's **attention**.
   b) Getting her to **understand** you.
   c) Getting her to **appreciate** and **believe** you.
   d) And finally, getting her **to do** or **act upon** what you suggest.

In this sense, communication is the ability to persuade and convince others. It is a very important skill in successful selling and includes a good voice, the ability to listen and observe, appropriate speech and grammar, acceptable manners and gestures, effective planning and organization, and showmanship.

Determination and persistence

The number of sales a salesperson makes usually is directly dependent upon the number of calls she makes. Also, the number of calls will usually outnumber the sales, and in some cases the call-sales ratio may be as great as 5 to 1 or even higher depending upon the product or service being sold. In addition, several repeat calls on a particular prospect must often be made before a sale is achieved. To make and keep on making the large number of calls that success demands, a salesperson must possess a high degree of determination and persistence. She cannot allow herself to become discouraged and must continue her efforts until her objective is achieved. Not too many people can do this, for it is much easier to find excuses or to wait for buyers to come to them. However, such an approach will seldom work; for no matter how good your product or service might be, prospects generally will not beat a path to your door. Many other choices are usually available to the buyer, and the market for a given product is usually too competitive for this to happen. Consequently, the salesperson must work in a determined and persistent manner in order to be successful.

Self-starter

Being a self-starter means having the capacity to do things on your own with little or no supervision from others. The salesperson has a high degree of freedom, as she generally works alone, with little interference or supervision; and in certain types of selling, the salesperson is completely free each day to decide when she will work, where she will work, and what she will do. Many find this freedom to be one of the advantages of pursuing a career in selling. However, it also means that the person out in the field selling is responsible for supervising herself. Those who lack initiative or are incapable of disciplining themselves will fail as salespeople. The work of selling is demanding and involves considerable time and effort if one is to succeed. Consequently, it requires a person who can operate on her own with little or no supervision; a person who can organize and complete her own work schedules. In short, selling is a highly individualized occupation; and in order to succeed in it, one should have a high degree of personal initiative and be a self-starter.

Sense of humor

As previously discussed, considerable time and effort is often spent on calls which may never result in sales. Also, buyers, by what they say and do, can sometimes discourage or frustrate a salesperson. It is difficult and trying to operate in such an environment, and a salesperson without a sense of humor can easily be overcome by these circumstances. However, with a sense of humor she can see the lighter side of human nature and is less apt to take herself too seriously. She must learn how to live with frustration, how to be friendly in unfriendly environments, and how to adjust to discouragement and failure.

A sense of humor will, therefore, not only help her to survive, but will also help her to be a more likable person.

Creativity

All buyers tend to be different, and each sales situation requires a somewhat different approach. Furthermore, in an economy of increased competition, product qualities and prices tend to become more similar. In such an environment, the creative ability of the salesperson becomes an important factor in securing the sale. To be creative means being alert and looking for new approaches to solving persistent problems. It involves constant experimentation in an attempt to find new ideas to help and serve the buyer. Selling is an art of adaptation to varying circumstances, and there is a great need in today's marketplace for the creative salesperson.

Appearance

Much that has been written on appearance has been erroneous and based on individual prejudice. Salespersons vary in height, weight, and physical looks. To be successful, one does not have to be tall; to be trusted, one does not have to have blue eyes. More important than inherited physical traits are the actions the salesperson takes to keep neat, well groomed, and well dressed. Although successful salespeople will vary considerably in height, weight, and physical looks, almost all of them will be neat and properly dressed.

Good health

Good health is the most precious gift a person can possess. The salesperson should watch her diet, exercise regularly, rest a sufficient numbers of hours, and be careful not to abuse her body. Such care will prolong her life and also help her to be a more effective and productive salesperson.

Poise and composure

The person who has poise and composure is well controlled and well mannered. She does not "fly off the handle" and is able to "keep her cool" in trying situations. She is also tactful, and has an air about her that instills confidence and respect in those who observe her. Hence, poise and composure are qualities necessary not only to be an effective leader but to be an effective salesperson as well.

Sincerity and honesty

Sincerity means taking a genuine interest in serving the buyer. This is a quality that all prospects look for and attempt to measure in the salesperson. If the buyer feels that the salesperson is insincere, he will lack confidence in what the salesperson says or does. Accordingly, it will be extremely difficult, if not impossible, for the salesperson to convince the prospect that he should buy her product or service. Sincerity must be real and genuine. It cannot be faked, for prospects can consciously or unconsciously feel it. Honesty is closely related with sincerity and requires that the salesperson be truthful in what she says and does for the customer. It means being upright in your activities as a salesperson and selling as you would like to be sold.

Developing necessary qualifications

Some qualifications are easier to develop or teach than others. For example, a salesperson can learn about her product, can be taught how to dress well, can learn proper grammar, and how to speak effectively. However, developing such qualifications as creativity, sincerity, being a self-starter, and determination and persistence are extremely difficult to teach, and in some cases, even impossible to teach. These latter qualifications present more serious problems for sales managers, and continued training is necessary to develop or improve them.

 ## Indicate whether each of the following statements is true or false

1. The salesperson should worry about her problems
2. The most successful salespeople are sensitive to the feelings and interests of others.
3. Most customers are sold on the first sales call.
4. Most salespeople are carefully supervised and have set schedules and duties.
5. Successful salespeople learn one sales presentation and perfect it, and have little need to adapt to different buyers.
6. The necessary qualifications and characteristics for becoming a successful salesperson can all be taught to any individual.

Answer

1. False. The "right mental attitude" is to minimize worry and to concentrate on the positive aspects of solving problems.
2. True. Salespeople who have empathy, or the ability to analyze how others are reacting to what they are saying or doing, have a tremendous advantage in attempting to convince prospects of the merits of products and services.
3. False. It often requires several repeat calls before a sale is achieved, and in some cases the call-sales ratio may be as great as 5 to 1 or even higher.

4. False. Salespeople generally have a great deal of freedom and are not closely supervised. This means that they must supervise themselves and have a high degree of personal initiative.

5. False. All buyers tend to be different, and each sales situation requires a somewhat different approach. Salespeople must be creative, which means that they must be alert and look for new approaches to solving problems. Selling is an art of adapting to varying circumstances.

6. False. Some of them can, but others like creativity, sincerity, being a self-starter, and so on, are extremely difficult to teach, and in some cases, even impossible to teach.

CHAPTER 3

Selling as a Career

Selling offers many career opportunities, for there are many different types and levels of selling. A person can sell a product or a service; she can sell to wholesalers, retailers, or ultimate consumers; and the product or service she sells can be technical or non-technical. Methods for paying the salesperson are also more varied than in many other types of jobs. She can be paid on a straight commission basis, a straight salary, or a combination of these two methods with many variations. In many selling jobs, earnings are unlimited and geared to the ability of the individual. In general, salespeople will receive significantly higher salaries than other business workers, particularly after they have become established and built up a clientele.

Another very important advantage of selling is that it is one of the main roads for promotion or advancement within the company. This is generally true because selling is the only business function which generates direct revenue and profits. Accounting, finance, production/operations, general management, personnel administration, and other related business activities are all expense operations. However, nothing happens until the product or service is sold; and the success or failure of all these business activities are measured by what happens in selling. This is why it receives major attention and is the hub or pivot point of all business activity. ***Note:*** Selling is the most important function in business. Everything else (that is, accounting, finance, operations, and the like) is ***secondary***. In a nutshell, you have to have money to count.

Work in selling is varied, challenging, and interesting. There is continuous contact with many different types of people, and each sales situation is uniquely different. No two customers are the same, and most products and services are constantly changed and improved to meet the varying demands of the marketplace. Almost every day there are new challenges and opportunities which make the work of the salesperson very dynamic and interesting. She also gains considerable pride and personal satisfaction in representing a reputable company and in helping customers solve their problems.

A career in selling also provides considerable freedom and independence in comparison with many other types of jobs in business. A field salesperson does not automatically begin each day at 8 A.M. and end it at 5 P.M. Nor does she punch a time clock and work under the daily supervision of a boss. On the contrary, as discussed in Chapter 2, in many types of selling the salesperson has complete freedom in determining when she will work, where she will work, how long, whom she will call on, and what she will do. Of course, she must periodically report to a sales manager, and her performance is carefully evaluated. She is generally rewarded in proportion to her abilities.

Finally, a successful salesperson has a skill which is highly transferable and is in constant demand. If she can sell one product or service well, with a little training she is generally capable of selling other products or services. The need for selling is universal; for although buyers will vary, they still buy many of the same products and services regardless of where they live.

Disadvantages of selling

As with all types of work, selling has some disadvantages. Many people dislike the high degree of persistence and personal discipline which is necessary for success in selling. The job requires time, training, and the ability to shrug off rebuffs and disappointments, and many beginning salespeople do not have the necessary patience and determination to stay with it. There can also be uncertainty and insecurity in selling, for earnings are largely dependent upon the actions others take and the acceptance they give the salesperson. Competition is always a threat, and general economic conditions, such as unemployment or rising prices, can unfavorably affect the earning power of the salesperson. Some people, therefore, prefer a form of work which is more secure and stable.

In addition, some aspects of selling are lonely and monotonous. Sometimes great distances must be traveled, and the salesperson may be away from home for several days. Also, long periods of time are sometimes spent in waiting to see prospective buyers. Work in selling can be very discouraging, for in the majority of cases more sales will be lost than gained.

However, the advantages of selling certainly outweigh its disadvantages for many people, and it provides considerable opportunity for personal satisfaction to those who have the necessary ability and determination to succeed.

Types of selling careers

Selling jobs can be classified in a number of different ways. Selling may be characterized as part time or full time; or as to whether it involves negotiation or competitive bidding;

whether it is routine or creative; whether physical products or services are sold. Classifications may also be made according to the method of compensation - whether straight salary, commission, or salary and commission.

In characterizing sales duties, the nature of the buyer may be emphasized, particularly whether buying to consume or to resell. The buyers may be wholesalers and retailers who purchase for resale. They may be purchasing agents who buy materials which are processed and sold in a different form; or they may be ordinary people or professional people who use the product themselves.

Along these lines, the Sales Marketing Executives International, Inc. (**http://www.smei.org),** has developed the following six classifications:

1. *Consumer route.* The job of the consumer route person is to sell and deliver goods to a list of consumer customers. The products are usually such staples as milk, bread, and laundry.

2. *Business route.* Salespeople on a business route sell and deliver such products or services as office, factory, and store supplies, production materials, and so on to a predetermined list of business customers.

3. *Consumer specialties.* The salesperson of consumer specialties engages in door-to-door selling and handles such products or services as life insurance, household products, cosmetics, appliance, siding and insulation, and other related products. She often does "missionary" work.

4. *Business specialties.* The salesperson of business specialties operates like the consumer specialty salesperson except she sells products or services to business establishments and is likely to do more creative selling. These salespeople handle such items as office machines, business insurance, advertising, and management training services.

5. *Retail.* The retail salesperson does not go the customer; the customer comes to her at a fixed place of business where she sells goods or services over the counter. Items commonly sold in this manner are clothing, household furnishings, automobiles, and appliances.

6. *Industrial.* The industrial salesperson generally must have a technical or engineering training. She sells such products as heavy equipment, machine installations, and product supplies.

Still another common way of classifying the salesperson's job is according to the nature of her employer - whether a manufacturer, a wholesaler, a retailer, or e-tailor.

It can be seen that there are many different types of selling jobs. Even those selling jobs within the same category can vary greatly as to the level of work and training required. Hence, there is considerable opportunity in selling; and the area pursued will greatly depend upon to whom the product or service is sold, the salesperson's interests, her level of education and training, and her particular abilities.

Note: The Sales Marketing Executives International's Career Center is a comprehensive online resource, with everything from professional résumé services and expert career coaching to salary data and advice for achieving better work/life balance.

SMEI's Certified Professional Salesperson (SCPS)

SMEI's SCPS® certification program is designed to ensure that those completing the program have successfully demonstrated knowledge and understanding of the core competencies outlined below.

Foundation Skills

- Segmentation, Differentiation & Positioning , Self Knowledge/ Professionalism,
- Product/Company Knowledge, Communication/Listening Skills
- ***Planning***
- Goal Setting, Forecasting , Understanding Motives and Needs, Decision Influencers,
- Features/Benefits Preparation
- ***Executing***
- Qualifying Prospects, Negotiations, Overcoming Objections, Closing, Customer Relations Management (CRM)

Indicate whether each of the following statements is true or false

1. In general, salespeople receive higher salaries than other business workers, and in many cases there is also greater opportunity for advancement.
2. Salespeople have a skill which is highly transferable from one firm to another and is in constant demand.
3. Because the work is creative and rewarding, there are few disadvantages to salesmanship as a career.
4. There are many different types of sales jobs which vary greatly as to the level of work and the training required.

Answer

1. True. Salespeople often receive higher salaries because they generate direct revenue and profit, and this often leads to greater opportunity for advancement.

2. True. If a salesperson can sell one product or service well, she is generally capable of selling other products or services if she is properly trained. The need for selling is universal, so there is always a demand for skilled salespeople.

3. False. As with any job, selling has some disadvantages such as the discouragement of making many calls with no results, long-distance travel away from home, insecurity of earnings, and the need for persistence and personal discipline.

4. True. There has been a tremendous increase in the number of salespeople in our economy and in the kind of work they do. The sales job varies from over-the-counter retail sales to highly complex industrial sales. Each job requires different educational and skill requirements.

CHAPTER 4

Motivation and Consumer Behavior

Motivation is characteristic of all human beings to have needs and wants, which when unsatisfied lead to tensions or drives. These drives toward relief of the tensions created by unsatisfied needs furnish the motivation - the activation forces - that determine and explain consumer behavior.

To be effective in her work, the salesperson must be able to analyze and understand consumer behavior and the motives that underlie it. What influences a particular customer to buy a particular good or service? If the salesperson understands these motivating influences, she will be in a stronger position to sell. Strictly speaking, the salesperson does not sell a product or service, but rather she changes the consumer's mind about the product or service. The product and salesperson remain the same, and it is the buyer's mind that must be changed. People buy products for what they will do for them, not for the product in and of itself. It is necessary, then, to study the behavior of consumers and to determine why they buy.

A great deal has been written about consumer behavior in the past, and this vast subject can only be touched upon lightly in this brief chapter. There are also varying theories and philosophies regarding consumer behavior and researchers in this area are not in agreement.

No two customers are identical

The first thing to recognize about consumer behavior is that no two individuals are exactly the same. People tend to have differing degrees of traits such as optimism, confidence, aggressiveness, conservatism, and so on. Not only do people differ from one another, but also the same person can be different under different circumstances.

Changes in the weather, changes in time, and many other physical conditions can attract or distract a person's attention. How a person feels will influence her behavior. Whether she is happy or unhappy, alert or sleepy, relaxed or tense will greatly affect what she perceives and does. Her use of alcohol, drugs, or medicine can produce changes in her behavior. And such incentives as praise, recognition, and reward usually will elicit a greater degree of response. Under varying conditions such as these, the salesperson should carefully analyze the total selling situation to determine the best approach to use.

Basic kinds of motives

Although the terminology varies and there is no general agreement on how many basic motives there are, authors in this area generally see the consumer responding to three basic types of motives. The first of these classifications is **physiological**. These motives are related to the physical needs of the body and include those arising out of sex, hunger, thirst, and the desire for comfort. The second is **psychological**, motives are largely subjective and include such motives as pride and fear. And the third is **sociological**. These motives are related to a person's social status, including motives arising from the urges or needs for conformity, recognition, and prestige.

Some authors have pointed out that motives can be arranged as a hierarchy, with those needs the consumer regards as most important, and will try to satisfy first, at the top and the others that can wait listed in turn below. The psychologist Abraham Maslow saw five levels of needs, which he listed in ascending order as follows:

1. Physiological needs.
2. Need for safety.
3. Need to belong, to love and be loved.
4. Desire for esteem and status.
5. Need for "self-actualization."

Maslow interpreted the need for self-actualization as a desire to find and fulfill the true self to the highest degree possible. He realized that this need came later in the hierarchy of needs after the others had been met.

Primary, selective, and patronage motives

Motives can also be classified as **primary**, **selective**, or **patronage**. A **primary** motive is related to those particular factors which motivate a person to choose one general type of product or service over another. For example, a person may simultaneously wish to purchase a new shotgun and storm windows. However, she usually doesn't have a sufficient amount of money to purchase both; consequently she must choose one over the other. In the case of the family person, although she wants to buy a new shotgun, she may decide that it is more important and sensible to buy storm windows for her home. Such considerations as the comfort of other family members, reduced heating bills, and increased value of her home may cause her to choose the storm windows over the shotgun and are referred to a primary buying motives. They relate to the type, kind, or class of product or service that will be purchased. **Selective** motives, on the other hand, are those that determine the consumer's choice of a brand. Once she has decided to purchase storm windows, she must next decide on the particular brand. Finally, **patronage** motives come into play. They involve decisions regarding the particular retailer or dealer from whom the product or service will be purchased.

Product motives

Consumer choice can also be influenced by the physical qualities or psychological attractiveness of the product. Such factors as design, color, size, quality, package, or price of the product can greatly influence or motivate the purchaser. For example, in designing packages, curved lines and fancy packages are generally thought to appeal to women, while straight lines and more functional packaging is considered more appropriate for products sold to men. With reference to color, red will normally attract more attention than green. And in promoting the cool taste of a cigarette, green and blue colors are frequently used.

The size of the container can also be an important motivating factor. Many shoppers select a larger size container because they can usually get more for their money by buying in larger quantities and it reduces the numbers of shopping trips. In addition, with our higher standard of living there is an increased emphasis on quality, but at the same time the product must be competitively priced. All of these factors can influence the purchase of a product, and they vary from one person to another. Product motives may also be thought of as economic or rational, as in the considerations of package size and price discussed in the preceding paragraph, or they may be classified as emotional. These classifications will be treated further later in the chapter.

The type of product being sought also influences consumer behavior. For example, such products as cigarettes, bread, meat, fruits and vegetables, gasoline, and toothpaste are classified as **convenience** goods. These products are frequently consumed on a daily or weekly basis, are available in many stores which are located near the consumer, are competitively priced, and are generally intensively advertised - particularly national brands.

Shopping goods, on the other hand, are such items as dresses, sport jackets, appliances, furniture, and automobiles. These products (in comparison with convenience goods) are consumed less frequently, are available in fewer outlets which are generally located further away from the consumer, and have greater variances in quality and price. The unit value of these products is also higher and often represents a sizable investment -- particularly in the case of purchasing an automobile, furniture, or a major appliance. Consequently, the consumer plans these purchases more carefully and will usually compare or do considerable shopping before a final decision is made.

Specialty goods are products which have very special and unique characteristics. The consumer generally will "go out of her way" to purchase such products, and usually is reluctant to accept substitutes. A certain blend of pipe tobacco, an exceptionally fine camera, pastry products which are made in a special way, and rare woods which are available only from a certain area of the country are examples of products which are classified as specialty goods. In summary, the salesperson should know the particular classification of her product and what effect its characteristics might have on influencing consumer behavior.

 ## Indicate whether each of the following statements is true or false

1. Most products are bought by consumers rather than sold by salespeople.
2. Salespeople may use the same basic appeal to everyone because most people have the same needs.
3. Researchers do not agree on how many basic buying motives there are.
4. Consumer choice is influenced by other factors besides the sales talk.

Answer

1. True. Strictly speaking, salespeople do not sell products or services. Rather, the consumer buys them. Therefore, it is necessary to understand consumers and why they buy.
2. False. People not only differ from one another, but the same person may react differently under different circumstances. Salespeople must vary their appeals according to the circumstances and needs of each customer.
3. True. Although there is no general agreement about buying motives, it is believed that at least three are basic: physiological (needs of the body), psychological (such as pride and fear), and sociological (the need to belong).
4. True. Consumer behavior is influenced by the product itself (design, color, size, price, package, and so on), by the type of product (convenience, shopping, or specialty good), and by the information provided by the salesperson.

Positive versus negative motives

When the salesperson emphasizes benefits or satisfactions that will be obtained from buying the product, she is emphasizing the positive approach. On the other hand, if she refers to a problem which the consumer wants to eliminate or avoid, she is using a negative approach. In selling life insurance, the salesperson can emphasize the retirement benefits -- this would be positive motivation. Or, she could emphasize the negative approach by referring to the financial difficulties a widow would have if her husband died and were inadequately insured. In selling a tire, the salesperson can emphasize the positive by referring to its trouble-free qualities and the long mileage it will give. Or she can emphasize the negative by pointing out the dangers of traveling at high speed and having a blowout. The negative approach is based on problems and fears. Both approaches are effective, depending upon the product or service being sold and the consumer's particular circumstances. However, recent research has revealed that a person generally responds more favorably to a positive appeal than to a negative one.

Basic versus acquired wants

Motivation can also be analyzed from the standpoint of basic versus acquired wants. Almost everyone has the same basic wants, and they are generally uniform for all human beings. Psychologists differ as to the number of basic wants they identify, and the following ones are representative of those most frequently mentioned.

Love

Each of us has a basic need to love and to be loved by others. The urge to appeal to the opposite sex plays a major role in our lives and influences our actions as consumers. A person also is concerned about the welfare of those she loves and usually assumes the responsibility for caring, protecting, and providing for them. Many parents not only provide a home for their children, but also labor to put them through college and even "help them out" in later life.

Food and shelter

Food and shelter are absolute essentials for living. There is a great range of differences in these needs varying from a dish of rice to a sirloin steak and from a simple hut to a stately manor. Nonetheless, we need food to live and work, and shelter to protect us from the elements.

Safety and security

A person wishes to avoid or eliminate anything that endangers or threatens her life. This basic urge manifests itself by her purchasing all forms of insurance, and in protecting herself and others through laws, support for police and fire protection, and other governmental services.

Achieve and accomplish

Most people strive to achieve and be recognized for something. They desire to be proud of what they do or accomplish. Attention, praise, and prestige are important motivating factors in our lives. In all things she undertakes, a person basically wants to succeed rather than fail. She constantly seeks new challenges and is motivated by a strong desire to master them. Climbing a mountain, conquering space, breaking records, and fulfilling one's ambitions are common examples of this basic want.

Approval and acceptance

It is common for all of us to seek approval and acceptance by others. We generally try to avoid criticism and ridicule. Our need for approval, therefore, causes us to conform and imitate, rather than to deviate from social convention.

Leisure and relaxation

In addition to working and achieving, a person also seeks rest, relaxation, pleasure, and fun. The increase in her leisure time and increased pressures of living have greatly influenced this need. Hundreds of recreational and vocational opportunities are available to her including golfing, fishing, hunting, surfing, skiing, reading, watching sports events, gardening, and many other activities.

Need for health and survival

Maintaining good health is a major concern of a person, and she will normally do everything in her power to avoid death. She also seeks to be free from fear, frustration, and pain. Millions of dollars are spent each year to research to find cures for common diseases and to lengthen her life. To live a long and happy life is a wished goal of almost everyone.

Acquired or learned wants are further refined, and therefore become secondary or selective wants that vary with the person's background and cultural environment. Every individual has the basic need for play and recreation, but the specific form it takes will vary considerably. For example, one person may fulfill this want by staying at home and reading a book. Another may attend a baseball or football game, and still another may fulfill this want by going on a lion hunt in Africa. Hence, the basic wants are common to all people, but the acquired wants will be different.

Emotional versus rational motives

As discussed in connection with product motives, consumer behavior can be viewed as being either emotional or economic or rational. Emotional motives are generally those which are based on feelings, are impulsive, and are not carefully planned in advance. Rational or economic motives, on the other hand, are more likely to be based on objective analysis and carefully planned. Examples of emotional motives would be those based on satisfaction of the senses, preservation of the species, love, pride, fear, emulation, sociability, acceptance, curiosity, and so on. Examples of rational motives would be those based on factors such as economy, efficiency in operation, durability, dependability, and others.

Difficulties in analyzing motives

In order to sell effectively, the salesperson usually must be able to determine the motives of her potential customers. Sometimes this is relatively easy to do, but at other times it may be extremely difficult. For example, a person may not be aware of the true reasons why he is interested in purchasing a particular product or service. A buyer may tell himself and the salesperson that he wishes to buy a new car because his old one is costing him too much for repairs. However, the real reason may be that he feels inferior and wishes to impress a certain young lady by buying a new car. The salesperson must realize that stated reasons are not always the real reasons. A person may sometimes believe he knows why he is interested in buying a particular product or service, but actually he is unaware of his true motives; or in some cases he may be aware of his true motives, but is unwilling to disclose them. How many women would admit that they were buying a new dress in order to attract the attention of men? Or how many men would admit that they use a certain product in order to give them more masculinity? Thus, the salesperson must understand human behavior and be careful in interpreting what the buyer says.

Finally, the salesperson should remember that it is often a combination of motives with varying priorities that motivate people to buy. Two housewives will buy a vacuum cleaner to keep their homes clean. However, in addition to this basic need, one bought the cleaner because it was like the one her mother had, and she also liked the salesperson because he reminded her of her own son. The other woman bought the cleaner because it was easy to handle, and it was also a better one than her neighbor had. Buying motives can vary greatly, and often no two people will buy a particular product or service for identical reasons. The salesperson should be constantly aware of this and should adapt her presentation to the prospect's particular motives whenever possible.

Theories of motivation

There are three basic theories of buyer motivations. The first is the "*mental-states*" theory, which maintains that the buyer's mind passes through successive stages during the buying process. These stages generally are "attention, interest, desire, action and satisfaction." The second is the "*appeal-response*" or "*buying-decisions*" theory, which maintains that the buyer makes a number of separate decisions in response to the appeals or stimuli presented by the salesperson. The third theory is called the "*problem-solution*" theory. This theory states that the wants, needs, or problems of the buyer should be the salesperson's frame of reference; and she gears her presentation to showing how her product or service will fulfill these wants or solve these problems. According to this latter theory, the salesperson does not sell a product or service but rather she sells solutions to problems. Therefore, the more benefits her product can give, the more likely she is to make the sale.

Regardless of which theory the salesperson may accept, she should recognize that there are different theories for analyzing motivation, and new discoveries are made each year which will help her to better understand the consumer she serves.

 ## Indicate whether each of the following statements is true or false

1. Psychologists agree that an individual generally responds more favorably to a positive appeal than a negative one.
2. People have basic wants that are uniform for almost everyone, but they also have acquired wants that vary considerably from individual to individual.
3. In order to determine why a customer wants a product, the salesperson has only to ask the customer directly.
4. People always have a major reason for buying a product that is clear in their mind.

Answer

1. True. Salespeople are usually more successful when they stress positive benefits, such as the satisfactions received from using a product, than they are when they dwell on negative factors, such as the dangers or problems resulting from not using the product.

2. True. An individual has certain basic wants such as approval, comfort, food, and mastery over obstacles, safety, and survival. She also has acquired or learned wants. A salesperson must determine how she can satisfy her customers' acquired wants as well as her basic wants.

3. False. Salespeople must realize that the reasons given by a customer for wanting a product are not necessarily the real reasons. The salesperson must look for hidden reasons in order to fully satisfy the customer's needs.

4. False. It is often a combination of reasons that motivate people to buy. These reasons are complex and difficult to analyze. A salesperson must be flexible and try to plan her presentation to meet the prospects' different motives.

Perception

Perception is an important factor affecting the behavior of consumers. It is the process of becoming aware of something through the senses of seeing, hearing, touching, tasting, smelling, and internal sensing. In relating to her environment, each person's needs, cultural background, past experiences, mental readiness, and motives will have an effect in determining how a given stimulus is perceived, even though the stimulus is the same in all cases. For example, a jackknife may be perceived by a youngster as a toy, by her mother as an object for possible injury, and by the minister as an instrument which promotes violence and killing. How it is perceived greatly depends upon who the perceiver is and her particular frame of reference. No two persons are likely to perceive the same stimulus in exactly the same way. Each individual sees what she wants to see, making perception a subjective and individualized process.

Perception is also selective, for often we are unable to comprehend or interpret all the sensations that converge on the senses at any given time. When a person looks down an aisle in a supermarket, she does not see the hundreds of items that are actually present. This is because the human mind generally is unable to absorb everything at once, and it selects those items which are of immediate importance. In addition, perception is generally of short duration. When we listen to a particular piece of music, we may respond to it very strongly; but when it is ended, our attention is quickly diverted to other things, and the music fades from our minds.

Finally, perception is a summarizing experience. Consumers receive many varying sensations and put them together into a single, meaningful whole. For example, the brand name, special features, price, and many other factors will all be considered by a consumer in deciding whether she will or will not purchase a particular product. No two persons are identical in what they see or do, and being familiar with some of the basic processes of perception will help the salesperson to relate more effectively with the customer.

Consumer attitudes

An attitude may be loosely defined as a person's state of mind, feeling, or disposition toward something. Such terms as belief, feeling, opinion, inclination, and bias are often used synonymously with attitude. Attitudes are also formed by a person's personal experiences in life, influences exerted by others, and the particular environment in which she lives. Consumers are not born with a given set of attitudes, for they are developed and formed as one lives.

Attitudes have a tendency to persist because of past experiences, agreement or harmony associations, and relating one factor with another. An illustration of conditioning by past experience would be when a person responds unfavorably to purchasing a new shirt made of a new synthetic fiber because she was dissatisfied with one previously purchased. This can happen even if the new synthetic fiber has been improved and is superior to the earlier one. Associations that are in agreement or harmony take place when the consumer responds favorably to a particular salesperson because she (the salesperson) is in agreement with the consumer's attitude. For example, if the consumer prefers conservative clothes and the salesperson also has conservative tastes, the consumer is more likely to respond favorably to the salesperson. An example of the effect of relating one factor with another is a situation where the customer judges the whole store and all its merchandise on the basis of a single unpleasant experience with a sales clerk.

Factors causing attitudes to change are contradictory influences, strength or intensity of the experience, multiple syndromes of circumstances, and emphasis of a particular factor. An example of an attitude changing because of contradictory influences is when a very thrifty and conservative bachelor buys an expensive, flashy car because her girlfriend liked it and he wishes to impress her.

The strength or intensity of an experience can cause an attitude to change. An illustration of this is when a person who is completely indifferent to the dangers of smoking suddenly changes her mind because of a heart attack.

Or the consumer may have an attitude unfavorable to the purchase of a particular product but reverses her attitude and makes such a purchase because of a multiple syndrome of circumstances. The circumstances may be that the product catches her eye, a friend strongly recommends it, almost everyone is currently using it, and she is influenced by a highly persuasive salesperson.

Changes in an attitude can also occur when there is emphasis of a particular factor or when the consumer makers a decision to purchase on the basis of a single dominant factor which is stronger than several others combined. For example, a person may have definite attitudes regarding the brand name, color, material, and price she wishes to pay for a sport jacket but chooses one almost entirely on the basis of its style because of the attention it will attract. A change in the product or service, new ways of perceiving the product, a change in the type and/or amount of information available on the product, a change in how the product idea is communicated, and a change in the importance of the product are additional factors which can influence and change consumer attitudes.

Learning

Another important dimension of consumer behavior is learning. There are varying definitions, but generally the essence of learning is that it involves a change in a person's response or behavior, Human responses can either be learned or unlearned. Examples of unlearned responses are breathing, blinking your eyes, and crying. All other responses not based on instinct or reflexes are learned. Forgetting, which is the loss or fading of a thought that was previously in the mind, is another aspect of learning. Because of forgetting, it is often necessary for the salesperson to repeat or reinforce and idea if she is to be effective in influencing the consumer to buy a particular product or service.

Although learning takes place in different ways, the three basic processes involved are **stimulus**, **response**, and **reinforcement**. In order for a stimulus to take place, and object generally must be perceived, and motivation must also be present. The object may be physical or non-tangible. For example, the customer may be stimulated by such physical things as a particular product, a given size or quantity, its color, or its style. In other cases she might be stimulated by such intangibles as the service she receives or the prestige value of the product. In addition to perceiving the object, the customer will also be motivated by love, security, safety, or many other motives.

The response is an action or reaction resulting from the stimulus and can be either physical or mental. Responses vary in speed, frequency, and/or in the nature of the response. Research has also shown that learning tends to increase as the speed, the frequency of correct responses, and the reward of the response increases.

Reinforcement is the third basic factor in the learning process. Definitions vary among authors, but it may be loosely defined as a condition which increases the probability of an identical favored response. It can also be defined as a rewarding or satisfying situation which helps to stimulate the same response. There are three laws of reinforcement -- the law of **effect**, the law of **exercise**, and the law of **readiness**. The law of effect refers to repetition of a satisfactory response. If an association is formed between a stimulus (a product advertisement), a response (going to the store to buy it), and reinforcement (experiencing satisfaction with the product), the connection of these three processes is generally strengthened by repetition.

The law of exercise relates to a form of conditioning. If the customer experiences the same stimulus a second time, she responds more quickly and with less difficulty because of her satisfying experience in the first instance. It is similar to a runner who continues to improve her performance as she continues to exercise and practice.

The law of readiness refers to the customer's ability and willingness to solve a problem. If she has the ability and willingness to learn, effective learning generally can take place. And conversely, if these two qualities are absent, then little or no learning will occur. As previously discussed, learning is any change in a person's response or behavior. Applying it to selling, then, means that the salesperson must be able to change customers from negative or indifferent positions to positive ones if she is to be successful in making sales.

Dyadic interaction

There has been considerable research on qualities necessary for success in selling and on consumer behavior. However, most of these studies have been made exclusive of each other, and only in recent years has there been research on the interaction between the customer and the salesperson. Such research is referred to a "dyadic interaction" where two separate units are treated as one. It is an integrated analysis of the roles played by both parties in a sale. These studies also focus attention on the transaction itself and on such factors as content of the transaction, average length of the transaction, and when and where the transaction takes place.

Other related variables also are isolated, controlled, and studied. Some of these studies have shown that the more alike the customer and salesperson are in such factors as age and economic and social background, the greater is the probability for a sale. Other studies have indicated that dependent persons tend to favor more assistance from the salesperson in arriving at purchase decisions, while independent persons tend to prefer a minimum of assistance. As far as the sex of the purchaser is concerned, some of these studies have shown that males are more likely to respond favorably to aggressive salespeople than are females. Research of this kind is relatively new, and the findings should not be accepted as hard-and-fast conclusions which will always apply. However, such studies emphasize the many variables that must be analyzed in order to better understand the interaction between the customer and the salesperson.

？ Indicate whether each of the following statements is true or false

1. If two persons witness the same robbery of a bank, they are both likely to give identical accounts of the event.
2. A "straight" college professor may buy mod clothes because of a multiple syndrome of circumstances.
3. The three basic factors in the learning process are stimulus, response, and readiness.

4. Dyadic interaction research has produced some hard-and-fast conclusions regarding the interaction between the customer and the salesperson.

Answer

1. False. No two persons are likely to perceive the same stimulus in exactly the same way. Two witnesses to the same event often tell vastly different stories based on different perceptions.
2. True. The clothes may have caught his eye, a friend (or his wife) may have recommended them, almost everyone else at the university was wearing them, and he was influenced by a highly persuasive salesperson.
3. False. They are stimulus, response, and reinforcement. Readiness is one of the three laws of reinforcement.
4. False. The findings should be regarded as tentative at best, but relevant variables are being identified and future research is likely to produce more useful knowledge.

CHAPTER 5

Information on the Company, the Product, Competition and Advertising

"An ounce of prevention is worth a pound of cure" and how carefully a salesperson prepares for a sale will greatly determine how successful she will be. It is, therefore, important for the salesperson to know certain things about her company, her product, her competition, and current advertising before approaching the prospective buyer.

Company information

The salesperson serves as a personal representative of her company and should be well informed about its history, growth, and development. How has it grown since its beginning? What are its particular policies which distinguish it from its competitors? What is its present size and sales volume? What is the present price of its stock? What new product lines and improvements have been made, and what are its future plans and objectives? What are its attitudes and practices relating to current social issues such as pollution and civil rights? The salesperson should also be familiar with central and regional operations of the company, where they are located, plus the name of major executives and some background information on each of them. More importantly, the salesperson should know the company's policies and procedures as related to prices, discounts, delivery, credit, and service.

Product information

It is the salesperson's responsibility to be well informed on her product. She should know how her product is made and be fully informed on its different styles, models, sizes, and prices. Markets are constantly changing and most products are periodically redesigned and improved; keeping up to date on product knowledge is, therefore, a never-ending process. The sources for obtaining current information on her product are many. They include company manuals and brochures, training programs, advertisements, magazine and newspaper articles, discussions with other salespeople, trade and association reports, and other related sources.

A salesperson should also know the major selling points and disadvantages of her product or service and specifically how it differs from other products or services. For instance, how can it fulfill varying needs and problems of prospective buyers and what are its limitations? Every product or service has some limitations, and the salesperson should know what they are and be prepared to clear up common misunderstandings and answer objections. Furthermore, the salesperson should be informed on current product research and advertising. Such material can be shown and/or distributed to prospective buyers and serves as an effective tool for selling. In addition, the salesperson should know about operating and servicing her product, as well as the guarantees and warranties that are offered.

Information on competition

Being informed about her own company and product is not enough; the salesperson must also be well informed about the products or services offered by her competitors. Prospective buyers will frequently refer to competitors' products or ask specific questions about them. The salesperson should, therefore, know the advantages and drawbacks of each competitive product and be prepared to explain and prove the particular merits of her product in comparison with specific competitor products. Furthermore, she should have some idea about the sales volume and market share of each competitor and know their basic policies and procedures as related to prices, discounts, credit, and service. Rather than directly criticizing the products of her competitors, the salesperson should emphasize the advantages of her own product.

Advertising and selling

Advertising is addressed to the masses, while personal salesmanship is geared to specific individuals. Advertising is also designed to presell the product or service, and personal salesmanship is used to follow up with more detailed information and to close the sale. Effective advertising and personal salesmanship work together to achieve the same objective -- namely, to stimulate sales. Each is important, and these two functions must operate together as a coordinated effort.

It is the salesperson's responsibility to keep abreast of all current advertising conducted by her company. She must know the content of each ad and when it appeared. She should be able to explain to dealers the uses and advantages of advertising and show them how it can help them move the product off their shelves after she has sold it to them. The following are some common points she can mention: (1) advertising increases demand for the product or service. A dealer can sell advertised products more quickly than unadvertised ones because the consumer is presold to a certain extent and is already aware and informed about the product; (2) advertising creates faster turnover of inventories, and faster turnover means lower operating expenses and greater profits; (3) through advertising and branding, consumers can identify quality products that they wish to buy again. Such identification also helps to establish a good reputation for the dealer who handles the product; (4) advertising not only helps the customer to identify products, but also provides her with valuable information about their quality and performance.

Advertising also helps the salesperson in many ways:

1. It develops customer interest and helps to presell products and services.
2. The salesperson can use advertising to emphasize and reinforce sales points she mentions in her presentations.
3. Advertising reaches the masses and serves as a means for securing new leads and contacts. Thus, it often reaches some people whom the salesperson, because of distance or other circumstances, is unable to contact.
4. Sometimes the salesperson is unable to call on all her customers as often as she would like, and advertising helps her sell between calls.
5. The presentation of new ideas and information through advertising stimulates interest and increases motivation in the salesman herself.

To use company advertising effectively, the salesperson should carry copies of current advertisements to show to prospective buyers. She should also be well informed on her company's total advertising program and be able to explain its uses and benefits to the buyer. Sometimes a buyer will ask questions on how she can tie her efforts in more effectively with the advertising campaigns, and the salesperson should be able to give the buyer appropriate suggestions. It is also the salesperson's responsibility to get the buyer to use any direct mail, point-of-purchase, or cooperative space advertising her company provides. Finally, she should obtain the buyer's reaction to, and suggestions concerning, her company's advertising in order to make it more effective.

It is recognized that the salesperson's knowledge of her company, her product, competitive products, and current advertising will vary with her experience and training. It sometimes takes months and even years to prepare for a particular sales position. Furthermore, it is a continuing process, for markets and products are constantly changing. To keep abreast of these changes is an important responsibility of the salesperson, which will greatly determine her success or failure.

 **Indicate whether each of the following statements is true or false**

1. The salesperson serves as a personal representative of the company and should be well informed about its history, growth, and development.
2. It is enough that a salesperson thoroughly understands her company and its products in order to be successful.
3. Once a salesperson learns all about her company's products, she can concentrate on other problems and not study her own products any further.
4. Advertising is an aid to the salesperson, and she should carry copies of current advertisements to show to prospective buyers.

Answer

1. True. A salesperson should know all about her company, especially its pricing policies, discounts, delivery, credit, and other services.
2. False. Being informed about her own company and products is not enough for a salesperson. She must also be well informed about the products or services offered by competitors in order to discuss the relative advantages and disadvantages.
3. False. Most products are periodically changed and improved, and keeping up to date on product knowledge is a never-ending process.
4. True. Advertising helps the salesperson by increasing demand for products, establishing a good company image, providing consumer information, reaching people the salesperson cannot, and stimulating and motivating the salesperson herself. The salesperson should use these ads to support her presentation. The salesperson should also provide feedback from the customer to make future ads more effective.

CHAPTER 6

Credit, Pricing and Discounts

Credit and collection

The three C's of credit. Many products or services are purchased on a credit basis, and the salesperson should be familiar with the policies and procedures for granting it. Credit is permission to buy a product immediately and to pay for it later. Moreover, credit is a privilege, not a right, which means that the buyer is morally and legally responsible to pay for the products or services he receives.

In opening a personal credit account for the buyer the salesperson must answer the following three questions: ***Can the buyer pay*** for what she purchases? ***Will she pay***? What ***amount of credit*** should be given?

To answer their questions the salesperson must have information about the buyer's capital, capacity, and character, commonly referred to as the "three C's of credit." Capital relates to the buyer's financial position. We need to have a picture of her assets, liabilities, and net worth. Capacity pertains to the buyer's weekly or monthly income. And character applies to the buyer's personal integrity, honesty, and past dependability in paying her bills. All three of these factors must be carefully analyzed to determine the buyer's ability and willingness to pay, as well as the amount of credit she will receive.

Sometimes a salesperson will be so eager to sell that she minimizes the importance of credit. She may concentrate only on selling and look upon the collection of payments as management's responsibility. Such an attitude is harmful, because the salesperson's cooperation is needed if the company is to operate a successful credit program. She should remember that profitable selling is measured, not by the number of units sold or their total dollar volume, but by the total amount of money actually collected as well as the expenses involved in collecting it. The salesperson or personnel in the credit department should not be apologetic about asking for money owed to the company because it is only proper that a buyer should pay for the products or services she has purchased and used. If she doesn't, either the company or the salesperson, or both, will suffer losses.

Why customers don't pay. Failure to pay for a product or service will vary from one customer to another. Some of the common reasons are as follows:

1. The buyer does not understand or has been misinformed about the credit terms.
2. Sometimes the customer deliberately delays making her payments because she is unhappy with the product.
3. Sometimes the amount owed is very small, and the customer prefers to postpone payment until the amount is larger.
4. Some customers are habitually slow in paying their bills, and several notices must be sent before they will pay.
5. Customers are sometimes careless or forgetful.
6. Occasionally a person will run short of money because of unexpected circumstances. Maybe she overbought, maybe she was in an accident, or maybe she had an unusual opportunity to buy something else.
7. A change in economic conditions or a sudden decrease in earning power can sometimes be the cause for delinquent payments.
8. Finally, there are a small percentage of people who are simply dishonest and deliberately avoid paying their bills. The policies and procedures for correcting these problems will vary from one company to another, and the salesperson should be thoroughly familiar with them.

Indicate whether each of the following statements is true or false

1. Buying on credit is a right guaranteed to every person.
2. "Capital" relates to the buyer's financial position.
3. A buyer's ability and willingness to pay, as well as the amount of credit she can receive are determined by using the "three C's of credit."
4. Most customers who don't pay their bills are dishonest and do so deliberately.

Answer

1. False. Buying on credit is not a right but it is a privilege, which creates a responsibility to pay for the product or service purchased.
2. True. It refers to the buyer's assets, liabilities, and net worth.
3. True. The "three C's of credit" do determine a buyer's ability and willingness to pay, as well as the amount he can receive. Capital (financial position), capacity (income), and character (the buyer's personal integrity, honesty, and dependability) are the "three C's of credit."

4. False. There are many reasons why customers may fail to pay their bills such as misinformation about credit terms, habitual slow payment, carelessness, unusual circumstances, changes in the economy, and so on. Only a small percentage of nonpayers are dishonest per se.

Pricing

Price definitions

There are many different ways in which the word price is used, and the salesperson should be familiar with them if she is to serve the customer in an effective manner. Following are some of the terms commonly used:

List price

This is a quoted or published price from which buyers are normally allowed discounts.

Net price

The net price is the final price after all discounts and allowances have been deducted.

Zone price

For some products, prices are equalized for certain zones or geographical areas. Many manufactured food products are priced in this manner.

Basing-point price

Under this system a price is determined from a given location or base point. There are both single and multiple basing-point systems. A single basing-point system is used when a manufacturer ships to buyers in different locations but charges all of them the same price regardless of the distance involved. A multiple basing-point system, on the other hand, is used when several production centers are used as basing points and chargers are based on actual distances from each production center.

Postage-stamp delivered price

This pricing method is used when a company wishes to sell its product or service at the same identical price throughout its entire market.

Fair-trade price

This is a price established by contract between a manufacturer of a branded product and a wholesaler or retailer. The manufacturer decides what the minimum price will be and the wholesaler or retailer may not sell below this established price.

Guaranteed price

When prices are falling, buyers may ask the seller for protection against any further price decreases that might occur prior to the time the product is either used or resold to the ultimate consumer.

F.o.b. price

This abbreviation means "free on board" a railroad car, a ship, a plane, or a motor truck. Under this system the seller assumes the transportation charges to a given shipping point, and the buyer incurs the costs beyond that point. If the term f.o.b. destination is used, it means that the seller incurs the transportation charges from the seller's place of business to the final destination point.

F.a.s. price

This abbreviation means "free alongside" and is used on overseas shipments. The seller agrees to pay the transportation charges for getting the goods within reach of the loading cranes, and at this point title passes to the buyer.

C.i.f. price

This term means, "cost, insurance, and freight" and is used in export selling. It includes cost of the goods, transportation costs to the seaport, charges for ocean shipping and insurance, and other charges for landing goods at a foreign port. Title passes to the buyer when the seller delivers the goods to the common carrier.

? Indicate whether each of the following statements is true or false

1. Under a single basing-point price system all buyers of a product would pay the same price (including freight).
2. Postage-stamp delivered price means that all buyers of a product or service would pay the same price (including freight).

3. On goods shipped f.o.b. destination the buyer would incur all the freight costs.

4. On goods shopped f.o.b. shipping point the seller would incur all the freight costs.

Answer

1. True. The freight charge is the same for all buyers regardless of the point from which the goods were shipped.

2. True. This pricing method is used when a company wishes to sell its product or service at the same price throughout its entire market.

3. False. The seller incurs all the transportation charges on goods shipped f.o.b. destination.

4. False. Title passes to the buyer at the shipping point. Thus, she incurs the transportation costs beyond that point.

Major laws regulating prices and trade practices

The salesperson should also be familiar with the following major laws.

Sherman Antitrust Act of 1890

The purpose of this act was to prevent monopolies and restraint of trade. Criminal penalties were provided for violators and aggrieved persons were entitled to recover three times the amount of losses suffered as a result of the violation.

Pure Food and Drug Act of 1906

This act made illegal the adulteration and misbranding of food and drugs. It was strengthened and extended to include cosmetics and therapeutic devices by the Food, Drug, and Cosmetics Act of 1938. Today, foods, drugs, devices, and cosmetics entering interstate commerce, as well as production operations, are inspected. Penalties for violations of the act include seizure of illegal goods, injunctions to restrain unlawful shipments, and criminal prosecution of those responsible for the violation. In like manner, the Meat Inspection Act, passed in 1907, empowered the federal government to inspect and certify processed meat.

Federal Trade Commission Act of 1914

This act established the Federal Trade Commission, which was given the power to investigate and to issue cease and desist orders. The act declared "unfair methods of competition' to be illegal. The FTC regulates a broad variety of business practices that may tend to hurt other businesses or consumers.

Clayton Act of 1914

The Sherman Antitrust Act of 1890 was weak and had to be reinforced by the Clayton Act. This act broadened the latitude of antitrust prosecution by defining practices as unlawful "where the effect may be to substantially lessen competition or intent to create a monopoly." In other words, the government no longer had to produce proof of actual monopoly or conspiracy. Four particular situations were singled out to make the law more specific. They were certain types of price discrimination, tying and exclusive agreements, inter-corporate stockholdings, and interlocking directorates. These practices are not illegal per se, but only if they substantially lessen competition.

Tariff Act of 1930

This act stipulated that the country of origin must be clearly indicated on imported articles or on the containers which enclose them.

State fair-trade or resale price maintenance laws

These laws are aimed at excessive price cutting and legalized resale price maintenance contracts through which the manufacturer is able to set or control the price at which her product is sold by distributors. In 1931 California enacted the first of such laws. It proved ineffective because retailers who did not sign contracts undercut those who did. It was reinforced by an amendment incorporating a "nonsigner's clause," which made the law apply to nonsigners and signers alike. The California law and the nonsigner's clause were widely adopted by other states, so that by 1941 all but a handful of states had fair-trade laws. But by 1967 the laws were made inoperative or repealed by court decisions in all but 16 states.

Robinson-Patman Act of 1936

The primary purpose of this act was to protect small business by regulating price discrimination on products bought by retailers. It held that "It shall be unlawful . . . to discriminate in price between different purchasers of commodities of like grade and quality where the effect of such discrimination may be substantially to lessen the competition or tend to create a monopoly, or to injure, destroy, or prevent competition."

Miller-Tydings Act of 1937

This act allowed manufacturers in interstate commerce to make resale price maintenance contracts which stipulated what the minimum prices would be at the retail level. At first the law was thought to be binding on nonsigners, but in 1951 the U.S. Supreme Court ruled otherwise. In effect this made the act of little help to national distributors, who would have to secure signed agreement with thousands of retailers if they hoped to maintain prices. (See McGuire Amendment.)

Wheeler-Lea Act of 1938

This act amended the FTC Act of 1914 to give the Federal Trade Commission specific authority to proceed against not only unfair methods in competition but also unfair or deceptive practices, including false advertising.

The Wool Products Labeling Act of 1939

This act requires that the percentage amounts and specific types of wool (such as virgin, reprocessed, or used wool) be clearly indicated on woolen products. Fibers or fillers other than wool must also be disclosed.

Antimerger Act of 1950

The purpose of this act was to prevent the lessening of competition by making it more difficult for large companies to acquire other large or even medium-sized companies in their own or closely related markets.

The Fur Products Labeling Act of 1951

The act states that such information as whether the fur is new or used, from what specific part of the animal it is obtained, and whether the fur is bleached or dyed must be clearly disclosed on the label.

The McGuire Amendment of 1952

This amendment to the FTC Act reestablished the legality of price maintenance agreements in interstate commerce and made it enforceable among nonsigning dealers if one in the state had signed such an agreement. It enables manufacturers to enforce both minimum and maximum prices under the resale price maintenance provisions.

The Automobile Information Disclosure Act of 1958

This act requires that the following information be clearly posted on the window of all new passenger vehicles: suggested retail price, the specific price of all extra equipment and options, and transportation charges.

Unfair trade practice laws

Many states have recognized the dangers of predatory price cutting and have passed laws prohibiting unfair trade practices. These laws will vary, but generally they prohibit price cutting below a specified level that usually is set at approximately 6 percent above the invoice price.

The Hazardous Substance Labeling Act of 1960

This act requires manufacturers of household products which contain toxic, corrosive, or flammable substances to give clear and adequate warnings on the labels of such products.

Fair Packaging and Labeling (Truth-in-Packaging) Act of 1966

This act attacks deceptive packaging as well as labeling that is misleading or insufficiently informative. It requires that the label state new contents of the package. It does not, however, provide for the standardization of weights and measures in packages, something that needs to be done if the shopper is to be able to make quick comparison of values when shopping.

Consumer Credit Protection (Truth-in-Lending) Act of 1968

This act bans methods or stating credit terms that tend to hide the true annual rate of interest. It requires the lender to make clear the actual cost of credit by expressing it in writing in dollars and cents and showing it as a percentage figured as a simple annual rate on the amount borrowed, taking into account unpaid balances. Thus the borrower is now informed that what he might earlier have thought was, say, a 6 percent annual rate is really 18 percent on unpaid balances. The law does not establish maximum interest rates.

Magnuson-Moss Warranty Act of 1975

This act provides minimum disclosure standards for written consumer product warranties; allows the FTC to prescribe interpretive rules in policy statements regarding unfair or deceptive practices.

Consumer Goods Pricing Act of 1975

This act prohibits the use of price maintenance agreements among makers and resellers in interstate commerce.

Telephone Consumer Protection Act of 1991

This act establishes procedures to avoid unwanted telephone solicitations; prohibits marketers from using an automatic telephone dialing system or an artificial or prerecorded voice to certain telephone lines.

Children's Online Privacy Act of 1998

This act requires the FTC to formulate rules for collecting online information from children under age of 13.

In addition to the above laws, many of the cities in the United States have regional Better Business Bureaus and local Chambers of Commerce. Although these organizations do not have the power to make actual arrests, they offer assistance to the consumer and businesspeople by investigating complaints of fraud or unfair business practices reported to them and by establishing guidelines for ethical business practices.

Discounts

The salesperson must also be familiar with discounts which will vary with the company and type of product or service being sold. Some of the common types are these:

Cash discount

The purpose of a cash discount is to encourage and reward early or prompt payment. A common cash discount is 2/10/net 30, which means that the buyer will be given a 2 percent discount if she pays her bill within 10 days from the date of invoice, and that otherwise the full amount must be paid within a 30-day period.

Trade or functional discount

Some companies sell their products to different types of distributors and will grant them trade discounts depending upon their trade classification and the services they perform. Trade discounts vary greatly, are quoted in series, and are related to the specific operating expenses of each trade. For example, a manufacturer of auto accessories may offer a 40 percent discount to wholesalers, 30 percent to dealers, and a 25 percent discount to chain stores.

Quantity discounts

There are savings in buying in large quantities, and this discount is designed to reward such purchases. They may be stated in a number of ways with typical bases being: (1) the number of total units purchased; (2) the dollar value of the order; (3) the size of the package ordered -- which usually encourages sales that allow the seller to reship the merchandise in the original containers; (4) bonus goods or "free deals," wherein the customer receives free merchandise or extra units depending upon the quantity ordered.

Advertising discounts

A schedule of advertising allowances may be granted to the buyer, depending upon the amount and type of merchandise she buys. However, advertising allowances are restricted by the Robinson-Patman Act, which prohibits the granting of such allowances unless they are offered on proportionately equal terms to all competitor buyers.

Early-order discounts

These discounts are designed to encourage the buyer to order early in the season.

Group discounts

These are discounts which are given to a group of buyers who pool or combine their purchases into a single order. The seller must also be able to justify such discounts on the basis of actual savings in selling to a group.

c.l and l.c.l

The abbreviation "c.l." means "carload" -- that is, a full carload for which a higher discount is given. "L.c.l." means "less than carload," a shipment that carries a lower discount.

"Mixed car-lot" discounts

This is a common discount in the building material industry which allows the buyer to buy in smaller quantities rather than full car or truck lots of one product. Under this system, the buyer receives a balanced assortment of products and still receives a carload price.

There are many other types and a form of discounts, and it is the salesperson's responsibility to know the ones that her company and her competitors offer.

? Indicate whether each of the following statements is true or false

1. The Sherman Antitrust Act of 1890 limits violators to civil penalties and the aggrieved person to recovery of the actual amount of loss suffered as a result of the violation.
2. The Clayton Act of 1914 was passed because the Sherman Antitrust Act was too weak.
3. Many laws directly affect the salesperson and her freedom to quote prices and meet competition.
4. The purpose of cash discounts is to give better prices to select customers.
5. The Wool Products Labeling Act of 1939 requires that the specific types of wool used in making woolen products be clearly indicated on tags or labels attached to these products.
6. The Fur Products Labeling Act of 1951 requires information as to whether the fur is new or used and whether the fur is bleached or dyed without reference to the specific part of the animal from which the fur was obtained.

Answer

1. False. Criminal penalties are provided for violators. Also, aggrieved persons are entitled to recover three times the amount of losses resulting from the violation.
2. True. Under the Clayton Act the government no longer had to prove actual monopoly or conspiracy. If "the effect may be to substantially lessen competition or tend to create a monopoly," the government could successfully prosecute.
3. True. Salespeople should be especially aware of the provisions of the Clayton Act, state fair-trade laws, the Robinson-Patman Act, the Wheeler-Lea Act, and the unfair trade practice laws. Those who deal in items sold on credit terms should understand fully the Truth-in-Lending Act of 1968.
4. False. Cash discounts are used to encourage and reward early payment of bills. A common discount is 2/10/net 30, which means the buyer will be given a 2 percent discount if he pays within 10 days from the date of the invoice, otherwise the full amount must be paid within 30 days.
5. False. This act also requires that the specific percentage amounts be indicated, as well as other fibers or fillers, which are used in making the product.
6. False. This act also requires information indicating the specific part of the animal from which the fur was obtained.

The Selling Process and Prospecting

To better understand the job of a salesperson and how it should be managed, the selling process can be broken into a series of steps. Each step in the process may not be required to make every sale, but the salesperson should become skilled in each area in case it is needed. The steps are shown in Figure 7.1.

Figure 7.1: The Selling Process: Steps Involved

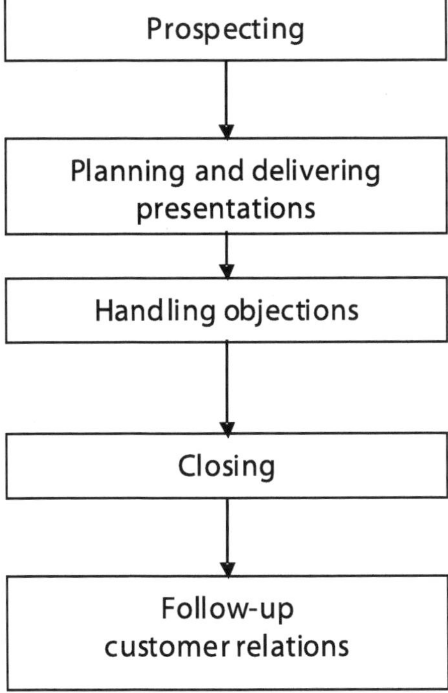

Each of the steps is discussed in the present and later chapters.

Prospecting

Success in selling depends more and more on ability to find new prospects in the face of increasing competition. In most situations competition is too keen to allow a salesperson the luxury of waiting for prospects to come to her. She must take the initiative, for sales do not just happen - they are the result of careful planning and hard work. Prospecting is one of the major means for increasing sales and earnings.

Or course, the amount of prospecting that must be done will vary with the product or service being sold. A retail salesperson generally does little or no prospecting, as the prospect usually comes to the store in response to its advertising. In selling life insurance, however, the salesperson usually must go into the field and locate prospects.

Considerations for selection prospects

Not everyone is a good prospect, and the salesperson has to be able to select those who are prospective buyers. We shall discuss some of the factors that aid selection in the following paragraphs.

The prospect should have a **definite need or want** for the product or service. Such a need can be specified by the prospect at the outset or may be an unrecognized one which the salesperson creates or uncovers. In either case, a real need must exist or be developed, for selling a product to someone who doesn't need it is detrimental to both parties. Successful selling is dependent upon repeat sales, and repeat sales will follow only if the customer needs the product and is satisfied with it.

The prospect should have the **ability to pay** for the product or service. Sale of a product to someone who cannot pay for it is a disservice to the prospect, to the company, and to the salesperson. In the case of the prospect, she will be forced to do without something else in order to pay for the product, or she will experience embarrassment and resentment when steps are taken to collect the money she owes. For the company, it can mean a loss from failure to collect the amount due. The salesperson also suffers because selling to a person who is unable to pay may require considerable effort in trying to collect the money and may also reflect unfavorably on her judgment in selling to such a person.

The prospect should have the **authority to buy**. If the prospect has no power or authority to make the purchase, the salesperson will often waste valuable time in contacting them. This does not mean, however, that the salesperson should completely ignore someone who does not have the authority to buy. For example, and assistant to a purchasing agent may not have the authority to buy, but she may exercise considerable influence in helping the purchasing agent to make her decisions.

It is important that the salesperson **be able** to **approach the prospect under favorable circumstances**. For example, the president of a large corporation would very likely not react favorably to a beginning salesperson and might not even be willing to see her. Also, a prospect should not be approached at an inconvenient time or place, or when she is very busy and the salesperson's appearance amounts to an annoying interruption. Care should, therefore, be exercised in approaching the prospect at the time and place that will be favorable to the sale. Needless to say, there will be some prospects who are always too busy to see the salesperson. However, the salesperson should generally respect the schedules and activities of her prospects.

Finally, the prospect should be **eligible to buy**. In some cases salespeople can sell only to wholesalers or retailers. It is obvious that in such instances she would be wasting her time if she were to select prospects who were ultimate consumers. In the case of a vacuum cleaner salesperson, she should make her presentation to the mother who is eligible to buy rather than to her teen-age daughter who may have nothing to say about the purchase.

Prospecting methods

As previously discussed, prospecting methods will vary with the type of product or service being sold. Following are some of the methods which are commonly used.

The "cold-canvas" or "cold turkey" method

Under this method the salesperson calls on any of the persons or companies within a certain class or group. She does not carefully preselect her prospects. Instead she goes from door-to-door and depends upon the law of averages to give her sales. It is sometimes a discouraging type of selling because many persons are not at home or in the office when the salesperson calls without an appointment. This method of prospecting also has a high refusal rate.

Lists

To avoid the "hit-and-miss" results of cold canvassing, lists are sometimes used. These lists are carefully prepared with reference to sex, age, marital status, income, occupation, and so on, and help to identify those persons who might be interested in purchasing a particular product or service. Often these lists are purchased from commercial companies. They are frequently used for direct-mail advertising with the salesperson following up on the inquiries received.

Company leads

Often prospective buyers will contact the company directly, and such information is given to the salesperson who follows up on the call. Or managers of auto and appliance agencies will usually instruct service and repair personnel to inform the salesperson of any persons who have older cars or appliances in need of repairs and are likely to qualify as prospective buyers.

Company advertising

Companies may receive inquires from their advertising which are relayed to the salespeople. Sometimes a free gift is offered to the prospect who requests information about the product or service. Then a salesperson delivers the gift and further explains the product.

Friends and acquaintances

Sometimes a salesperson's friends and acquaintances will serve as a good beginning source of prospects. Also such persons as neighbors, relatives, fraternity brothers, business associates, people from whom the salesperson buys, and others are excellent sources for locating other prospects.

The customer reference method

Under this method the salesperson attempts to obtain the names of additional prospects from persons she has interviewed or who have purchased from her. With others helping her, this simple method can provide the salesperson with a continuous supply of prospects.

The testimonial method. This method is similar to the customer reference method. It differs, however, by selecting persons who are well known and/or influential in the community. The salesperson keeps in close contact with these people and uses their names and assistance in selling to others.

Group prospecting

Sometimes the salesperson can make arrangements to give a group demonstration to clubs or service organizations. Or she can give demonstrations at the home of someone who is willing to sponsor her. Such products as cosmetics and household supplies are often sold in this manner, and the sponsoring party is usually rewarded with merchandise based on the number of persons who attend or the volume of sales made.

Surveys by junior salespeople

Some companies use junior salespeople to make surveys or canvasses of consumer demand. They seldom attempt to sell the product but instead pave the way for the experienced salesperson to make the actual presentation.

Sales spotters

These are persons who aid in prospecting by providing information on potential buyers. The associate receives cash or premium rewards from the salesperson if this information results in a sale.

Public exhibitions and displays

Many companies display their product or service at public exhibitions. Products usually displayed at such shows are automobiles, boats, sporting goods, computers, and equipment, furniture, and many other products. Company representatives pass out literature and explain the product at these exhibits. They also secure the names and addresses of interested persons which are given to the salespeople.

Personal observation

The salesperson frequently comes in contact with different people and different situations. If she is alert and keeps her eyes open, these circumstances can often help her to find persons who are likely to be good prospects.

In summary, there are many different methods for prospecting. Their use and effectiveness will vary with the product or service being sold, and the enterprising salesperson will attempt to use as many as possible to increase her sales.

 Indicate whether each of the following statements is true or false

1. Sales prospecting is the major means for increased earnings for many salespeople.
2. Everyone is a potential prospect for a sale and should be treated accordingly.
3. There is no one way of prospecting that is appropriate for all salespeople.
4. Group prospecting refers to the practice of groups of salespeople calling on people to persuade them to buy.

Answer

1. True. The amount of prospecting varies with the product or service sold, but in some fields, such as life insurance, prospecting is the key to success.
2. False. Only those prospects who have a definite need should be sold. Further, only those who have an ability to pay should be considered. The prospect should also have authority to buy, she should be approachable, and be eligible to buy. Prospecting, therefore, is a narrowing-down process of finding customers.
3. True. Some salespeople are most successful calling door-to-door, while others use commercially prepared lists. Company leads are also very effective, as are friends and acquaintances, referrals, and other such techniques. A salesperson should try many of these techniques to see which ones work best for her.
4. False. Group prospecting involves giving demonstrations or talks to various clubs or organizations who are willing to listen. This technique has been very effective in selling cosmetics, household supplies, and other such goods.

Additional considerations for effective prospecting

In addition to using the methods that have just been described, the salesperson should have an organized plan or system for identifying and evaluating prospects. She should establish a priority system for determining those that she will call on first, those she will call on second, and so on, and then arrange a schedule to carry out her program. She should also have goals or quotas for securing new prospects.

At the same time, she must be realistic in the quotas she sets. For if she spends too much time prospecting, she may not adequately serve the customers she already has and may consequently lose as many customers as she gains, or more.

Keeping good records and regularly following up on prospects is another aspect of good prospecting. It often requires several calls before a prospect finally becomes a customer. Therefore, the salesperson should record what happened on each visit and plan each succeeding call to bring her closer to consummating a sale.

The salesperson should also experiment with new methods and techniques -- particularly if she has called on the prospect several times and had been unable to make a sale. Effective prospecting should result in sales; and if it doesn't, then the salesperson should carefully reappraise her approaches and possibly consider other alternatives.

Last, but not least, the salesperson should always analyze her effectiveness in making a good impression or in creating a favorable attitude. Sometimes she seems to be using excellent methods and is working hard at it but has limited success. In such cases, it is often helpful to have another salesperson or sales manager accompany her on some field calls in an effort to help determine the cause of the problem. On the other hand, a salesperson should carefully examine a sale where she has been successful and see if the same methods will bring her success in comparable situations.

Guidelines for using the telephone

The telephone can be an important aid in prospecting and in increasing the productivity of the salesperson. However, it should be used as a supplement to -- not a substitute for -personal selling. It can be effectively used to make sales; to schedule appointments; to communicate new developments related to the product, prices, and promotion; to promote goodwill; to handle problems; to contact the home office; and for prospecting and preapproach work. Its many uses should not be overlooked, for it can save time, reduce travel costs, allow for more and faster contacts, enable the salesperson to call on isolated accounts, and help to provide the customer with continuing service.

When using the telephone, the salesperson should attempt to select prospects in accordance with some predetermined criteria. If possible, only those who have the potential for becoming customers should be called. The call should also be carefully planned and organized. She must not use the telephone for idle conversation and gossiping. Instead, the salesperson's objectives should be carefully determined, and the call should be designed to fulfill them. Nor should the telephone conversation be too long. Its primary use is to make appointments, to determine the prospect's general needs and wants, and to secure basic information.

At the beginning of the conversation, the salesperson should identify herself and the company she represents and briefly explain the purpose of her call. Throughout the conversation the prospect's name should be mentioned when appropriate. More involved and detailed information should generally be presented by the salesperson in person. It is helpful to keep brief notes on what has been discussed. An amazing amount of information can be covered over the telephone and the salesperson sometimes is apt to forget some of the points that were mentioned.

It is also important for the salesperson to remember that the buyer cannot see her. Her voice and words are the only tools she has for developing a good impression, and the prospect will do some visualizing on the basis of what she hears. The salesperson must, therefore, be familiar with basic techniques for effective speaking including speaking at a proper speed, using the right words and phrases, maintaining a satisfactory volume, and speaking in an organized and understandable manner. Furthermore, the salesperson must be a good listener and should learn how to detect through listening the various feelings of the buyer. It is also helpful to the salesperson to have someone periodically listen to and comment on her telephone effectiveness. Sometimes the salesperson can have an annoying manner which causes the listener to react negatively. She should, therefore, seek and evaluation from others in an attempt to improve her performance.

Finally, the salesperson should remember that many buyers find it easier to say no to a salesperson by telephone than they would in a face-to-face situation. For this reason, it is not wise to attempt to close most sales by telephone.

Direct-mail selling

Direct-mail selling can supplement personal selling activities. It can be used to secure direct orders, to obtain inquiries and solicit appointments, to invite prospects to the store or firm for a demonstration, to encourage customers to use the credit they have established, and to thank customers for their patronage. Some common forms of direct-mail advertising are sales letters, postcards, circulars, flyers, and inserts.

First, to be effective, direct-mail selling should be based on a prospect list that is current and up to date. The needs and status, as well as the mailing addresses, of consumers change, and a good list should accurately reflect the changes that have occurred from one period to another. Second, the direct-mail program should be carefully planned and organized. This includes consideration of details such as the appeal that will be used, the layout and appearance of the mailing piece, the timing of the mailing, the costs, and the total number of mailings. The third step is to acknowledge all inquiries immediately and to have a plan for determining which ones will be answered by a personal call, by telephone, by mail, or which ones will be delayed until additional information is received. Finally, every direct mail program should be evaluated to determine the relationship of its costs to sales generated. Direct-mail selling can be an effective means for increasing sales, and its success is largely dependent upon how carefully it is planned and organized.

? Indicate whether each of the following statements is true or false

1. A salesperson should give first priority to finding new prospects for her goods or services.
2. A salesperson should experiment with new prospecting methods and new sales approaches.
3. Telephone prospecting is an excellent substitute for field selling.
4. The most effective direct-mail list is one which has been effective in the past.

Answer

1. False. If a salesperson spends too much time prospecting, she may not adequately serve the customers she already has. A salesperson's first priority should be toward servicing her present customers.

2. True. If a salesperson is not happy with the number of sales she makes to prospects, she should try new approaches to increase her effectiveness and keep her presentation fresh.

3. False. Phone prospecting is a supplement to, not a substitute for, personal selling. It can be effectively used to schedule appointments; to communicate new developments, prices, and promotion; to promote goodwill; and to handle problems. Any phone call should be carefully planned, with specific objectives, before the call is placed.

4. False. To be effective, direct mail selling must be based on a prospect list that is current and up to date.

CHAPTER 8

Types of Sales Presentations and Considerations for Effective Delivery

Successful selling is based on presentations which are well organized and effectively delivered. Many things can go wrong during the course of a sales presentation, and advance planning is essential if the salesperson is to achieve her objectives. Such planning and organization not only aids the salesperson, but also saves time for both her and the buyer.

Types of sales presentations

There are three basic types of sales presentations. The first of these is the **standard memorized presentation** which covers specific selling points in a particular sequence and manner. Its advantages are that it insures that the complete and correct story will be told, provides the salesperson with prepared answers to questions or objections that will be raised, and incorporates the techniques used by successful and experienced salesperson. The style of presentation also has inherent weaknesses, such as sometimes being too mechanical and artificial. Its structure often makes it difficult for the prospect to participate in the presentation, and it is also very embarrassing if the salesperson forgets her place or lines. In addition, it cannot be used effectively if several products are being sold.

The second type of presentation is the **outlined presentation** which follows a basic outline but need not be memorized like the standard memorized presentation. Its key advantages are that it allows more give and take with prospects, it is more natural than the standard memorized presentation, and permits closer identification of the buyer's specific needs by giving her more opportunity to participate in the presentation. It is also more flexible and makes it easier for the salesperson to get back on course if she is interrupted. Its drawbacks are that the salesperson may wander and deviate from the basic selling plan and thereby fail to mention certain key points. Also, some salespeople may not be able to express themselves effectively when they speak extemporaneously.

The third type of sales presentation is the **program presentation**. It consists of a highly organized and comprehensive proposal written and illustrated after permission has been secured to make a thorough analysis or survey of the prospect's needs. This type of presentation is widely used in selling life insurance, industrial equipment, and other products and services which must be specifically tailored to the buyer. Its advantages are that it puts the emphasis on the specific needs of the buyer, it represents a more professional approach to selling, and it concentrates on proven absolutes, thereby avoiding often wasted time in exploring for the real needs and problems of the buyer. Its major limitation is that the salespeople may not be qualified to prepare a program. It is costly and time-consuming to prepare such programs, and some prospects may be reluctant or suspicious when such surveys are made.

It can be seen that each presentation has its respective advantages and disadvantages. Also, the type of presentation to be used will vary with the particular product or service being sold and the experience and training of the salesperson. Generally, the standard memorized presentation is adaptable for single-line products where the ability and experience of the salesperson is limited. The outlined presentation is more appropriate for multiple-product lines where a higher level of selling is required. And the program presentation is used for products and services which require a careful survey of the prospect's needs and problems.

? Indicate whether each of the following statements is true or false

1. The standard memorized presentation should only be used by experienced salespeople where several product lines are being sold.

2. The outlined presentation is more flexible than is the standard memorized presentation.
3. The program presentation is more closely tailored to the customer's needs than are the other two presentations.
4. The program presentation is superior for all situations.

Answer

1. False. It is most adaptable where the ability and experience of the salesperson is limited and only one product line is being sold.
2. True. It follows a basic outline but need not be memorized. It reminds the salesperson of points that should be made, but allows for more give and take with the customer.
3. True. This type of presentation involves a thorough survey of the prospect's needs and then shows her how these needs may be met.
4. False. Each presentation is designed for a given type of situation. But it can be disastrous to use the wrong type of presentation for a given situation (e.g. a memorized speech to sell insurance).

Considerations for effective delivery

In addition to being well organized, the presentation must also be effectively delivered if it is to be successful. What you say and how you say it are of equal importance. Following are some points to help make the presentation more effective:

Preparation

Before she even begins the sale, the salesperson should be well informed about her product or service and should also know as much as possible about the prospect. Each presentation in terms of content, organization, and pace should be specifically tailored to varying types of buyers. Some buyers are better informed or more critical than others. They differ on the basis of attitudes, income, educational levels, social status, and other factors. In regard to professional buyers, they often will have different policies or requirements relative to price, quality, and service. Whether she is selling to consumers or professional buyers, the salesperson should recognize these latter differences and gear her presentation accordingly.

Organization

The presentation should be effectively organized and some of the common patterns for discussing the product or service are:

a) According to the natural or sequential order in which the operations of the product or service normally occur.

b) By first mentioning the major points, then following up and filling in with the minor points.

c) By starting from the bottom and proceeding to the top, or from the front to the back, or from one side to the other side.

d) By organizing the presentation on the basis of a ranking of the prospect's buying motives.

Proper setting and showing

The product should be displayed in a proper setting. A salesperson selling a new car does not park it in a mud puddle in front of a dilapidated building. On the contrary, she displays the car in an attractive show window, and nearby there are comfortable areas where the buyer and salesperson can privately confer. The product should also be realistically shown and handled. For example, in selling a tie the salesperson should knot it and display it on a matching shirt or sport jacket. Proper lighting and comfortable surroundings are also important factors for effectively showing the product.

Show and demonstrate

Actions speak louder than words, and an actual demonstration not only helps to convince the prospect, but also helps her to visualize what the salesperson is talking about. Demonstrations can be used in selling insulation by having the prospect actually try to burn it in order to prove that it is fireproof; or in selling a radiator sealing compound by actually filling a leaking radiator to prove that the leak will stop. There are hundreds of instances where demonstrations can be used, and the salesperson should utilize them whenever possible.

Outline key points

When the salesperson is explaining key points, she can be more convincing by also outlining these points on a small card or piece of paper, In this way, the prospect both hears and sees what the salesperson is talking about. If a product has been lowered in price and the markdown represent a significant savings to the buyer, the salesperson, in addition to explaining this point, could also illustrate it in the following manner:

Original price	$75.00
Markdown price	-30.00
Savings	$45.00 or 60%

Such illustrating emphasizes the point and also helps the prospect to remember it.

Use of mnemonic words is also helpful in highlighting or outlining key points. For example, such benefits as comfort, appearance, performance, economy and service can be illustrated by the word CAPES.

Use charts, graphs, and illustrations

These visual aids should be used to reinforce explanations, for they facilitate understanding and help the prospect to remember. The adage that a picture is worth a thousand words certainly applies to selling, and the salesperson should use these aids wherever possible. Company advertisements and product training manuals serve as an excellent source for obtaining these materials. It is also relatively easy for the salesperson to construct some of her own charts and graphs, for in many cases they involve nothing more than simple drawings or a listing of major points.

Appeal to a maximum number of senses

The salesperson will always explain her product and service. She thereby automatically appeals to the prospect's sense of hearing. The senses of seeing, feeling, smelling, and tasting, however, are often neglected or overlooked. In selling pure Pennsylvania Oil, the salesperson can appeal to four of the five senses in the following ways:

- Hearing - She explains the superior lubrication qualities of such oil.
- Seeing - She shows the prospect the rich green color of the Pennsylvania Oil in comparison with the reddish tint which is characteristic of a lower quality oil.
- Feeling - She lets the prospect rub a few drops of oil between her fingers. Pure Pennsylvania Oil will be slippery, whereas a cheaper grade will have a waxier feel.
- Smelling - The pure Pennsylvania Oil will have a strong and pungent smell, and the cheaper grade will be almost odorless.
- Tasting - In the case of oil, it obviously is not appropriate for the prospect to taste it. However, with such products as food and beverages this is a highly effective appeal.

Indicate whether each of the following statements is true or false

1. What you say is far more important than how you say it.
2. There is more than one effective way to organize a presentation.
3. Actual demonstrations should be avoided because if they go wrong there is little, if any, chance for a sale.
4. You should appeal to only one of the prospect's senses to avoid confusing her.

Answer

1. False. They are of equal importance.

2. True. For instance, it can be organized according to the natural or sequential order in which the operations normally occur, by mentioning major points first, and so on.

3. False. Demonstrations are very effective and should be used whenever possible.

4. False. The more of her senses you can appeal to, the more likely the presentation is to be successful.

Use the benefit-proof technique

The salesperson will ordinarily mention several benefits that her product or service will give the prospect. This is something almost all salespeople will automatically do, but the highly successful ones will go one step further.

In addition to mentioning benefits, they follow up with respective proofs. For example, one salesperson might say, "Our tire will give you longer mileage." But the one who follows the benefit with a proof will say, "Our tire will give you longer mileage because it is a steel-belted radial tire and track tests have shown that such radials give better results than fabric belted tires. Here, let me actually show you the difference." Then she proceeds to show the prospect the difference between a steel-belted radial tire and a regular tire. All prospective buyers seek benefits -- that is why they are interested in buying a particular product or service. However, despite their interests and needs, many do not buy because they are not convinced of the benefits the salesperson mentions. To make the presentation convincing and relevant to the prospect, each major benefit should be supported with one or more proofs.

Make comparisons

Comparisons emphasize differences and similarities, and the salesperson should employ some of the following types.

Similes

A comparison can be made between qualities by using the words "like" or "as." For example, "Proper insulation is like wearing warm and comfortable clothing." Or, "This car consumes gas as a miser spends money."

Metaphors

These are like images, but the comparative word "as" or "like" is omitted. For example, "This car has the power of an elephant and the gliding comfort of a cloud." ANALOGIES. These wordings take the prospect from the known to the unknown. For example, if a woman is reluctant to buy a power lawnmower because she feels it will be too dangerous to operate, the salesperson might say, "Do you remember how frightened you were when you first began to drive? It is the same with operating a power lawnmower. You will no longer be afraid to operate it once you become accustomed to using it."

Listen and observe

A sales presentation is not a monologue, and the prospect should be encouraged to participate. Furthermore, you should not only listen to what the prospect says, but you should also observe the manner in which she says it. Does she speak softly or forcefully? Does she speak slowly or rapidly? Does she look away or directly at you? Does she reinforce her remarks with significant gestures? Does she speak in general terms or does she back up her comments with facts and figures? All of these actions and others should be carefully noted by the salesperson, for they can serve as important clues in determining how to structure the presentation.

Use language and terms that the prospect understands

The language and terms used in the presentation should be geared to the particular prospect. Any terms or processes that the prospect might not understand, particularly when selling a product or service, which is new or highly technical, should be carefully explained by the salesperson. The prospect must first understand what the salesperson is talking about before she can make up her mind to purchase it. In this sense, the salesperson should regard herself as a teacher who must carefully explain the "whys" and "hows" of the product or service she is selling.

Emphasize key words

Certain words can also help stimulate favorable responses from the prospect. This idea can be illustrated in the following statement: "Our service is used by people who become successful and advance to responsible positions." The key or emotionally packed words in this statement are successful and responsible positions because they refer to the goals of almost every executive. Or when the utensil salesperson says to the newlywed, "Just think how much easier it would have been for your mother if she could have purchased such utensils." In this instance the key word is mother, a word which generally has favorable connotations and powerful emotional values.

Use specific explanations rather than general ones

If it is an economical purchase, be specific and explain how economical it is in actual dollars and cents. For example, instead of saying the product is "economically priced," the salesperson can be more specific by saying, "This chain saw was originally priced at $179.95 and had been marked down to $134.95, which represents a 25 percent markdown and a savings of $45.00." General terms to be avoided are beautiful, better, excellent quality, comfortable, stylish, and other similar terms. To make the presentation more interesting and convincing, more specific explanations should be substituted for these general and often overworked terms.

Be enthusiastic and confident

It is important that the salesperson maintain her enthusiasm and confidence. It is difficult, if not impossible, for the salesperson to make a prospect enthusiastic about her product and confident about what she is saying if she herself does not feel this way. Let your feelings show you believe in your product and are even excited about it. Enthusiasm is usually catching, and it also helps to maintain the buyer's interest in the product.

Vary the presentation

As previously discussed, the presentation should be designed to fit varying types of buyers. At the same time, to help maintain the prospect's interest, the salesperson should vary the speed and volume of her voice. The organizational pattern, particularly with lengthy presentations, should also be varied to avoid making the presentation too mechanical and boring.

Avoid distracting mannerisms and poor appearance

Such mannerisms as long and nervous pauses, needless fidgeting, hands in your pockets, slumping in a chair, sitting on a desk, rattling coins, swinging a chain, smoking, and so on, are usually very distracting and annoying to a prospect. The salesperson should also be clean and properly attired in order to create a favorable impression.

Eye contact

It is difficult for the salesperson to instill confidence in the buyer if she nervously looks away or down at the ground. Hence, you should look at the prospect while you are talking. This does not mean staring the prospect down, for this is just as bad as looking away. However, looking at her in a reasonably steady manner with occasional glances at the product or other related objects is the correct way to maintain good eye contact. In addition to keeping her attention, good eye contact also helps the salesperson to better observe the buyer's reactions.

Control

The salesperson should solicit responses from the buyer and also try to involve her in various aspects of the presentation. However, it is important for the salesperson to maintain control throughout the presentation if she is to achieve her objectives. Too often a salesperson can become sidetracked by a dominating prospect; and when this happens, the prospect usually succeeds in convincing the salesperson that she (the prospect) cannot be sold.

Repeat and review

The salesperson should periodically repeat and review to make certain the prospect understands and agrees with her. The salesperson should not falsely assume that if the prospect says nothing, she automatically believes and agrees with everything the salesperson has said. On the contrary, the prospect may be quietly seething inside, or worse yet, she may not even be listening. Consequently, the salesperson should periodically pause to ask questions in order to determine if the prospect really understands and agrees with the points she has mentioned. Generally, it is good procedure to secure agreement on one point before proceeding to another.

Indicate whether each of the following statements is true or false

1. The highly-successful salesperson usually mentions benefits while other salespeople do not.
2. The salesperson should actually encourage the prospect to participate in the presentation.
3. Good advice to a new salesperson would be to use language the prospect understands, emphasize key words, use specific examples, be enthusiastic, vary the presentation, avoid distracting mannerisms, and maintain good eye contact during the presentation.
4. Two dangers in selling are that the prospect may say too little or too much.

Answer

1. False. Almost all salespeople automatically mention benefits, but highly successful salespeople follow this up with one or more proofs supporting each of the benefits mentioned.
2. True. The prospect's reactions during the presentation are important clues as to how to proceed. Thus, she should be encouraged to participate.
3. True. All of the points discussed can aid in making the presentation more effective.
4. True. If the prospect says too little she may not be listening or she may be seething inside. If she says too much she may take control of the presentation and convince the salesperson that she (the prospect) cannot be sold.

CHAPTER 9

Opening the Sales Interview

Objectives of the opening

There is an old saying, "Well begun is half done." The opening sets the stage for the remainder of the interview and greatly determines whether the salesperson will succeed or fail. Within a very short time the salesperson must make the prospect like her, determine the prospect's needs and problems, and determine and organize the approaches she will use for the remainder of the sale. This is no simple task, and its successful execution requires a great deal of alertness and skill on the part of the salesperson.

In accomplishing these objectives, the salesperson should be on time for the interview and should also be dressed in appropriate attire. She should approach the prospect with a friendly smile and handshake and introduce herself with a statement such as the following: "Good morning, Mr. Smith, I'm Jane Doe from the Central Equipment Corporation. You recently requested some information on our new conveyor belt, and I'm here to explain how it operates and how it can increase your profits. I appreciate this opportunity to talk with you. I know your time is limited, so I will be as brief as possible. I would like to begin by asking you some questions about your present operation . . . ," and so on.

Note that the salesperson has accomplished the following things in using this approach:

▶ She has started off on the right foot by being on time and being properly attired.

▶ She has established good rapport by smiling and introducing herself.

▶ She mentions the prospect's name and also mentions it before her own name.

▶ She identifies the name of her company.

▶ She explains the purpose of her visit.

- ▶ She expresses appreciation of the prospect's time and promises to be brief.
- ▶ She begins by asking some basic questions in order to identify the prospect's needs and problems.

In short, she begins by being friendly and continues by being well organized and businesslike. If executed properly, such an approach will help to make the prospect like and respect her. It also puts the emphasis on the buyer's needs, because the salesperson asks for basic information on the prospect's present operation. However, the salesperson should learn as much as possible about the prospect's operation before calling on her. She should also listen very carefully to what the prospect tells her; and at the same time, she should determine the organization and approaches she will use in the remainder of the presentation.

The salesperson's attitude and approach

In opening the sale, the salesperson should be calm, relaxed, and "optimistically confident." She should realize how important the opening is, for first impressions are often lasting impressions. A poor start makes it difficult to finish well. The opening also takes very little time, but what is accomplished during this period will largely determine the final outcome of the presentation.

Some salespeople are ineffective because they feel they are bothering the prospect, particularly if the prospect is busy at the time they call. This definitely is not the attitude to have, for if the salesperson feels this way, she will be handicapped at the start. If the prospect has a need for the product and it will help her to make or save money, the salesperson should have no reluctance to approach her but should do so with confidence and enthusiasm.

There are many situations where a salesperson will have little or no information about the prospect whom she encounters. For example, she may notice a new store being prepared for an opening and decide to call. Or a new buyer may have been assigned to an account which the salesperson already services, and she learns of this change when she arrives. In such cases, she should not automatically assume that she must postpone her call until she learns more about the prospect; it is appropriate for her to call on the prospect immediately. A prolonged delay in order to learn more about the prospect may result in losing the opportunity for a new or continued account because of faster action taken by a competitor salesperson.

Every salesperson should also guard against assuming that once a sale is made, it is no longer necessary for her to learn more about the customer. On the contrary, successful selling is an ongoing process. The salesperson should continue to assemble information as long as she calls on the account.

Things to avoid

In executing the opening, the salesperson should not resort to flattery or "honey-dripping" compliments in an effort to get the prospect to like her. If the prospect has done something which merits a compliment, then she should be complimented. Otherwise, such an approach should be avoided, because the prospect can easily detect insincerity.

Though the salesperson should be confident and in control of the interview, she should be careful not to dominate it. Customers generally do not like "cocky" and overly aggressive salespeople. They usually resent being "pushed around," and the salesperson who resorts to such high-pressure tactics will often only irritate and anger the prospect. Consequently, the salesperson should encourage the prospect to participate in the interview, and she should be genuinely interested in securing the prospect's comments and reactions.

The salesperson should not call on a prospect just for the sake of calling. There should be definite objectives for each call, and the salesperson should strive to fulfill them. There is no excuse for taking up the prospect's valuable time when the salesperson has no objective in mind.

 Indicate whether each of the following statements is true or false

1. A salesperson should begin preparing for a sales presentation long before she actually sees the prospect.
2. The opening sets the stage for the remainder of the interview and greatly determines whether the salesperson will succeed or fail.
3. As a salesperson, you should have the attitude that you are a problem solver and that you have something which will benefit the prospect.
4. An effective sales "opening" is to flatter the prospect so that she will like you.

Answer

1. True. The salesperson should learn as much as possible about the prospect's operation before calling on her.
2. True. Within a very short time, the salesperson must make the prospect like her, determine the prospect's needs and problems, and decide upon and organize the approach she will use for the remainder of the sale.
3. True. If the prospect has a need for the product and it will help her to increase earnings, the salesperson should be eager and enthusiastic in approaching her.

4. False. Only if the prospect has done something, which merits a compliment, should she be complimented. Such an approach generally should be avoided because a prospect can easily detect insincerity.

Making appointments

Some salespeople feel very strongly that making appointments is necessary, while others feel it is too much bother. Normally, the advantage of making appointments are that they avoid the likelihood of seeing the buyer when she is busy and an appointment gives the buyer time to prepare for the interview. The drawbacks of appointments generally are that they often make it easy for the buyer to refuse to see the salesperson and to put her off, and sometimes the weather or other circumstances will make it difficult to be on time or to keep an appointment. What use should be made of appointments is an individual decision, which will vary with the product or service being sold and the particular circumstances of the sale. Therefore, the salesperson should carefully study each sales situation and vary her approach according to the circumstances that prevail.

First-call obstacles

First calls usually are more difficult than subsequent calls because on an initial call the salesperson may not have all the information about the prospect that she needs. She should, of course, learn as much about the prospect as she possibly can prior to calling on her. An attempt should be made to learn what product or service she is presently using; what her specific needs and problems might be; her major personality traits; her interest and community affiliations; her age, educational level, income, occupation, and other related information which might be helpful in determining how to approach her.

However, the salesperson must realize that regardless of the information she has gathered about the prospect, she will often encounter certain obstacles on first calls. Many prospects have a fear of strangers which puts them on the defensive when a salesperson first calls on them. They may not give the salesperson a sufficient amount of time to tell the complete story about her product or service. Some prospects may state that they are too busy to talk with the salesperson, and others may simply indicate that they have no need for or interest in the product the salesperson is selling.

The salesperson should expect such reactions from the prospect when she makes the initial call and be prepared to overcome them. To do this she must be skillful in analyzing people and establishing rapport. She must learn how to gain the prospect's confidence by being friendly and demonstrating a sincere desire to help her. She must learn how to secure and maintain the prospect's attention by relating the presentation to the prospect's specific needs and interest. She must also know how to ask questions to which the prospect will respond. Experience will help the salesperson to become more successful in overcoming these first-call obstacles; but more importantly, success in doing so requires careful analysis and training.

 ## Indicate whether each of the following statements is true or false

1. A salesperson should dominate the interview and use high-pressure tactics if this seems necessary.
2. It is a good idea to call on a prospect occasionally just to say hello and maintain contact.
3. The first sales call is often the most difficult and requires special preparation.
4. Whether or not to make appointments is an individual decision which will vary with the product being sold and the particular circumstances that prevail.

Answer

1. False. Customers generally do not like "cocky" and overly aggressive salespeople, and the salesperson who resorts to such tactics will often irritate and anger the prospect.
2. False. The salesperson should never call on a prospect just for the sake of calling. There is no excuse for taking up the prospect's time when the salesperson has no objective in mind.
3. True. An attempt should be made to determine what product the prospect is now using, what her problems might be, her personality and interests, and other such helpful information. Experience will help a salesperson to become more successful in overcoming first-call obstacles.
4. True. Some salespeople feel very strongly about making appointments and others feel it is too much bother. There are advantages and disadvantages to making appointments; the salesperson should carefully study each sales situation and determine whether an appointment would be opportune or not.

CHAPTER 10

Handling Objections

Common causes for objections

Customer objections are a normal part of the sales process. The salesperson should expect them and be prepared to handle them. Objections will vary depending upon the particular buyer. Frequent underlying causes are:

1. The buyer lacks trust in the company or the salesperson.
2. The buyer has a natural resistance to change in her purchasing habits.
3. The buyer does not have the required financial capacity to make the purchase.
4. The buyer does not need the product or service.
5. The buyer needs more information or fails to recognize her needs.
6. The buyer assigns a higher priority to the purchase of other products.

Knowing the causes for objections will help the salesperson to do a better job in answering them. She should, therefore, carefully analyze the reasons behind objections before proceeding to answer them.

Common types of objections

Common objections can be classified further on the basis of price, product characteristics, the company or salesperson, bad service experience, and use of procrastination to delay or avoid making a decision.

Price objections are expressed in such terms as:

a) "The price is too high."
b) "I'm going to wait for a lower price."
c) "I don't wish to spend that much."

Product objections are often stated as:
a) "I don't like the style or design."
b) "I prefer a better quality."
c) "It's not appropriate for what I had in mind."

Company objections are characterized by comments such as:
a) "I don't like the business practices of your company."
b) "I prefer doing business with a company I know more about."
c) "I prefer trading with a smaller company."

Prospects may also often react negatively to certain **salespeople** because they have personality characteristics or do something which the prospect does not like. They may make the objections known in such candid comments as:
a) "I just can't trust you."
b) "I'd never buy from you because you're too high pressure."
c) "You just rub me the wrong way."

Objections based on ***bad service experience*** may be expressed in the following ways:
a) "You don't have a service representative in the immediate area."
b) "It takes too long to get service."
c) "You have a reputation for giving poor service."

Delay objections are mentioned in these terms:
a) "I wish to wait and look around a little more."
b) "I need more time to think it over."
c) "I would like to discuss it with someone else."

Considerations for handling objections

A positive attitude about objections will help the salesperson to handle them better. She should welcome rather than fear objections, realizing that they are normal and that they will help her to establish better rapport with the prospect. Such an attitude takes the salesperson off the defensive and gives her a greater degree of confidence.

The salesperson can take the initiative in minimizing objections by providing information which answers them before they are mentioned. She can do this if she understands how buyers generally feel about a product or service and why they raise particular objections. The salesperson should also know that the buyer will sometimes object simply because she wants to test the salesperson or wishes to secure further information to help her to decide. Every product or service has its disadvantages, and the salesperson should try to take the initiative in putting them in as favorable of a light as possible before the buyer brings them up as objections.

All objections should be carefully analyzed, especially to determine if the buyer is close to buying but is deliberately delaying a decision by presenting superficial objections. In such cases, the salesperson should know the prospect's priority of buying motives and gear her presentation accordingly. What she says and how she says it are of equal importance. It takes considerable skill, involving tact and precise timing, to be effective in answering objections. Moreover, the salesperson should reason with the prospect rather than argue with her. A sales presentation is not a debate, and the salesperson should answer objections from the buyer's point of view.

Before answering the objection, the salesperson should make certain she thoroughly understands the buyer's reason or reasons for objecting. Sometimes the salesperson is so intent on selling her product or service that she fails to listen to what the buyer is saying. Such an approach leaves the prospect unconvinced, and the objection will usually persist. Most objections are also raised or continue because the salesperson has not given the prospect a convincing explanation. She should, therefore, attempt to prove all the benefits she mentions by:

Demonstrating her product, appealing to all of the prospect's senses-not just seeing and hearing but touching, tasting, and smelling as well.

Comparing her product with other products.

Appealing to the prospect's needs and wants, showing how her product will satisfy them.

The use of the following materials will also help the salesperson to be more effective in handling objections: current advertising, charts, graphs, reference to guarantees and warranties, case histories, testimonials, current research reports, and so on.

 Indicate whether each of the following statements is true or false

1. The greatest fear a salesperson should have is a customer who raises lots of objectives.
2. It is often very effective to debate with a prospect over various objections to establish your position.
3. A salesperson would be wise to anticipate objections and have a ready answer for every one.
4. What you say in answering objections is more important than how you say it.

Answer

1. False. Objections are a normal part of the sales process and should be welcomed rather than feared.

2. False. A salesperson should reason with a prospect rather than argue with her. A sales presentation is not a debate, and the salesperson should answer objections from the buyer's point of view.

3. False. The method used for handling objections varies with the type of prospect being sold. The way the objection is answered depends on the circumstances related to the sale.

4. False. What you say and how you say it are of equal importance. The salesperson should be tactful.

Methods for answering objections

Recognizing that the method used for answering the objection will vary in accordance with the personality traits of the buyer and the particular type of objection that is raised, some of the commonly used techniques are outlined in the following paragraphs. Remember, too, that these methods may be used singly or in combination, depending upon the circumstances related to the sale.

Agree and qualify

This method answers the objection by first agreeing with the prospect, and then tactfully qualifying the answer or presenting additional information which offsets it. For example, the prospect may say, "I'm not interested in your product because I can buy it at a lower price from someone else." The salesperson replies, "Yes, this is true." However, the competitive products are of much lower quality and will last half as long as ours. (The salesperson should carefully explain and prove this statement. Therefore, you are really paying less for our product." From a psychological standpoint this is a highly effective method because the salesperson never directly disagrees with or contradicts the prospect.

Make the objection serve as a selling point

This method takes the very objection raised by the prospect and converts it into a selling point. For example, the prospect may say, "I don't care for this particular style because it currently is not being worn." The salesperson replies, "That's absolutely correct and that's why I'm showing you this particular style. It's the newest design, which soon will be very popular, and you can be one of the first to wear it." Or the prospect might raise the following objection in connection with a new type of printing press. "I don't believe I'm interested in your press because to my knowledge no one in this area is using one." And the salesperson might reply, "That's right, and that's exactly why I'm showing it to you. You have a bigger operation and are more progressive than the other printers in this area. Not only will it give you increased production and lower operating expenses, but it will also give you the opportunity to set a new standard in your area."

The effective use of this method is usually dependent upon the salesperson's being well informed about the prospect's buying motives and being able to determine what she really wants. In using it, the salesperson should also be very careful not to use high-pressure tactics or to offend the prospect.

Ask questions for further explanation

Sometimes the salesperson may not understand the nature of the objection and must ask for more information before she can give an effective answer. For example, the prospect might raise the following objection about a new systems program. "Your system is probably O.K for most companies, but it certainly won't work in mine." Before answering such an objection, the salesperson will have to have the prospect explain what she presently is doing and also determine why she believes the proposed system will not work. Sometimes the objection is not a truly valid one, and the salesperson can ask certain questions which will result in having the prospect answer her own objection. In buying a truck, the prospect may say, "I can buy a more stylish model from other dealers." And the salesperson in a polite and courteous manner asks, "Is style your most important consideration for buying a truck or are you more interested in performance and economy of operation?" A common reply by the prospect might be, "I'd like to have all three, but I know this isn't possible, so I'm definitely more interested in its performance and economy."

Agree that the objection is valid

Sometimes the objection raised by the prospect is a legitimate one. In such cases the salesperson should not be afraid to admit the objection, for no product or service is perfect in every respect. For example, the prospect may say, "I don't like an eight-cylinder car because it consumes more gas than a six-cylinder car." The salesperson replies, 'That's absolutely correct, but the eight-cylinder car also gives you more room, a more comfortable ride, and considerably more power." When the prospect mentions a valid objection, rather than dwelling on a futile discussion of its negative aspects, it is better for the salesperson to quickly admit it and then to shift to a discussion of its positive aspects.

Delay the answer

Sometimes the prospect will raise an objection before the salesperson has had an opportunity to explain her product or service. In such cases, the salesperson can politely say, 'That's a good point and with your permission I will answer it in a moment. But first it is necessary for me to explain how our product is made, and in so doing I know it will answer your question."

Politely deny that the objection is valid

The salesperson will seldom directly contradict the prospect, and this method should be used only if necessary and supported by the facts. However, the prospect will sometimes be completely wrong, or she will stubbornly persist in raising an invalid objection. In such cases, the salesperson should clearly and politely deny the objection. For example, the prospect may say, "I've been told that you sell this same product for 25 percent less in other areas." The salesperson can reply, "Someone has either misinformed you or you are confusing our company with another one, for we sell our product at the same price to everyone and have never deviated from this policy." The salesperson should speak in such a manner as to avoid antagonizing the prospect; and such an answer will usually be accepted. However, if the prospect still persists with such an objection, then the salesperson should ask for the name of the party who purchased the product at a lower price, and when and where such a transaction took place. She should also attempt to check it out immediately and tell the prospect that she will call back within one or two days with a complete report.

Pass up or ignore the objection

Sometimes the prospect is not serious about the objection she raises or she mentions an objection that doesn't warrant a serious answer. For example, the prospect might facetiously say, "I understand that you also supply a maid with every vacuum cleaner you sell." The salesperson might humorously reply, "We would like to, but unfortunately they're pretty hard to find these days."

 ## Indicate whether each of the following statements is true or false

1. If a customer makes a valid objection, the salesperson should agree with her and then offer an explanation.
2. Often an objection can be overcome by questioning the importance of the point.
3. Postponing the answer to an objection often gives a salesperson a chance to explain her product further.
4. A salesperson should never flatly deny an objection because it may irritate the prospect.

Answer

1. True. An effective technique for answering objections is to first agree with the prospect and then tactfully present information, which offsets it.

2. True. Sometimes the objection is not a truly valid one, and the salesperson may ask certain questions that will result in having the prospect answer her own objections.

3. True. Often the answer to an objection is contained in the sales presentation and may be brought up at the proper time if the prospect will agree.

4. False. In cases where the prospect is completely wrong, the salesperson should clearly and politely deny the objection, and if the salesperson speaks in a manner, which does not antagonize the prospect, the answer will usually be accepted.

CHAPTER 11

Closing the Sale

The close is the culminating stage of the sales process, the point at which the prospect decides whether or not she will buy. The salesperson should, therefore, be well informed and skillful in executing the close.

Coming difficulties in closing

The salesperson sometimes "tightens up" when she reaches the close, and the buyer can consciously or unconsciously detect this pressure. When this happens, the success of the sales is greatly impaired, for if the salesperson is to instill confidence in the buyer, she herself must be confident and in control of the sale. On the other hand, the salesperson may try so hard to close the sale that she uses high-pressure tactics and causes the buyer to become defensive. In either case-if the salesperson is too nervous or tries too hard to make a close—the sale will be seriously jeopardized.

Inadequate preparation and faulty presentations also make it difficult for the salesperson to close. If she has done a poor job of identifying the prospect's needs, or of showing her how her product or service fulfills these needs, her close will undoubtedly fail. A good close is dependent upon careful planning and effective execution of all stages of the sales process. In this sense, selling is comparable to a chain which is no stronger than its weakest link.

Successful closing also requires experience, constant analysis of closing attempts, and experimentation. Closing is an art which must be developed through practice. It is not developed overnight, and to be successful the salesperson must constantly work at revising and improving her closing techniques.

Considerations for effective closing

Timing

Many successful salespeople believe that the best time to attempt to close a sale is when the buyer has indicated in some way she is ready to buy. When that moment will occur will vary greatly. One prospect can decide that she wants a particular product or service on the first call, or before the salesperson has given her complete presentation. On the other hand, it may be necessary to approach another prospect several times, and each visit may require a very complete and lengthy presentation.

The proper time to close, therefore, depends upon the type of prospect being approached, the nature and extent of her needs (whether they are immediate or anticipated in the future, whether they are major or minor, and so on), and whether she has the financial capacity to buy. The salesperson should recognize that each buyer is different and her close should be specifically geared to the personality and needs of the buyer at hand.

Also, the close should not be looked upon as a separate part of the sale which occurs at the end of the presentation. On the contrary, what is done at the very beginning of the sale will greatly determine the outcome of the close. It is related to all phases of the sales process and is built and developed as the sale progresses.

Closing signals. Prospects may signal that they are ready or are not ready to buy by their expressions, participation in the presentation, or their comments. If the buyer frowns or looks confused, she generally is not ready to buy. In such cases, the salesperson must further explain the product and/or give more convincing proof that it will fulfill the prospect's needs.

The prospect's degree of involvement or participation in the presentation may also indicate her readiness to buy. For example, if a prospect tries on one particular sports jacket several times and looks at herself admiringly in the mirror, she is more ready to buy than the prospect who simply looks at the sports jacket and continues examining others. Or in buying an automobile, the prospect who examines everything very carefully, starts the engine, and asks to drive the car is usually more interested than the prospect who says or does nothing.

The most accurate closing signals, however, are furnished by the prospect's comments. What she says and the questions she asks are of cardinal importance in determining her readiness to buy. Seldom will she suddenly say, "I like it and want to buy, now just tell me how much it costs." Her comments are usually less direct and obvious and are more apt to be expressed in the following ways:

> *"What would my monthly payments be?"*

> *"How soon could you deliver this product to me?"*

> *"How much would you allow on a trade-in?"*

> *"It's more powerful and economical than my present boat motor, and I know my family would enjoy it, too."*

> *"It's priced right and is also better than anything else I've seen."*

Questions or comments such as these usually indicate that the prospect is genuinely interested in the product or service, and indirectly she may be telling the salesperson that she wants to buy. Sometimes a salesperson will become so engrossed in what she is talking about that she fails to look for or recognize common closing signals. Hence, she should carefully analyze the prospect's expressions, her participation in the presentation, and her comments in order to become more effective in closing the sale.

Frequency of trial closes

Very seldom will a sale be closed on the first try. More likely it will require further trial or attempted closes. These trial closes should also be varied, for to use the same method each time is often ineffective repetition which fails to bring the salesperson closer to closing. A good principle to follow is to try to close as often as good judgment dictates, and in a manner that will not irritate or antagonize the prospect.

Opportunities for attempting a close may occur at the following times in the sales process:

At the beginning or early in the presentation.

After a demonstration which is geared to a major buying motive.

After a major objection has been satisfactorily answered.

After the prospect has given a series of "Yes" answers.

After the first complete presentation.

After second, third, or fourth follow-up presentations.

After several calls.

Trial or preliminary closes

In as much as more than one close is usually necessary to make a sale, the salesperson will often use a trial, or preliminary, close which is designed to prepare the prospect for the final close and to determine what must be done to achieve it. Trial closes are usually necessary because:

The prospect is not completely ready for a final close.

There may be some questions about the prospect's priority of buying motives.

Additional information has to be presented or the prospect does not sufficiently understand the points that have been covered.

The salesperson may have failed to answer the prospect's objections satisfactorily.

Consequently, the salesperson should carefully plan the trial close and analyze it in terms of what has to be done to develop and execute a subsequent close.

Control of the sale

As previously discussed, the salesperson should control, but not dominate the sales interview. If the prospect takes over, closing attempts by the salesperson become extremely difficult, if not impossible. The salesperson should also be confident and determined, but at the same time avoid being "pushy" or using high pressure. In short, the salesperson should encourage the prospect to participate in the presentation, but the salesperson should always retain control.

Indicate whether each of the following statements is true or false

1. A salesperson should not stop until she has given her complete sales presentation.
2. The only way a salesperson can determine whether a prospect is ready to buy is to ask her directly.
3. Many times salespeople miss signals from the buyer which indicate that she wants to buy.
4. A salesperson often must make several attempts before she can actually close a sale.

Answer

1. False. The correct time to close a sale is when the buyer indicates she is ready to buy. Often a salesperson need not make a complete presentation or any presentation if the prospect is ready and willing to buy.
2. False. Prospects may indicate that they are or are not ready to buy by their expressions, participation in the presentation, or their comments.
3. True. Sometimes a salesperson will become so engrossed in what she is saying that she fails to look for or recognize common closing signals.
4. True. Very seldom will a sale be closed on the first try. More likely it will require two or more attempts.

Reserve selling points

The salesperson should not exhaust all the selling points that apply to her product or service before attempting a close. This is generally poor practice, because if the close fails after the complete presentation, she has nothing more to offer. It is like a quarterback who plays so hard during the first half of the game that he is unable to finish the second half. The salesperson should keep some selling points in reserve to serve as ammunition for subsequent closes.

Fit the item and quantity to the prospect's needs

The salesperson's chances for a successful close are greatly increased if what she is trying to sell is what the prospect wants and is in the quantity the prospect needs. If she suggests the wrong item or the right item in the wrong amounts, she will usually meet strong opposition, and her close will fail. The salesperson should remember that successful selling is based not on getting the prospect's first order but on securing the prospect's continued patronage. Her objective should be a satisfied customer who makes repeat purchases rather than the immediate purchase alone. Such an attitude will help the salesperson to sell the prospect only what she needs and in the proper amounts.

Methods for closing

There are many different methods for closing, and the methods chosen will depend upon the wants and personality of the buyer, the urgency of her needs, the number of closes that have been attempted, the number of times the prospect has been visited, and so on.

Following are some of the common methods that are used.

The alternative-choice close

This close does not ask the prospect if she wishes to buy but assumes that she **wants** to and is ready to **buy**. This method is designed to ask an alternative question which results in a sale regardless of the prospect's choice rather than asking a question which can be answered with a no. For example, the salesperson does not say,

> *"Do you wish to purchase this shirt?" Instead, she assumes that the prospect is ready to buy and gives her a choice by saying, "Do you wish to purchase the plain colored shirt or the striped one?"*

Other examples are:

> *"Do you wish to pay cash or charge it?"*

> *"Do you want us to deliver the product today or tomorrow?"*

> *"Did you wish to purchase one dozen or two dozen?"*

In using this method the salesperson must be reasonably certain that the prospect wishes to buy; otherwise it will appear that she is using high-pressure tactics.

Securing a series of acceptances

This method of closing the sale is executed by asking the prospect a series of questions to which she will answer yes. In this way a receptive attitude is developed, and it helps pave the way for a favorable response to the major questions (s) in the close. A clothing salesperson may implement this method in the following manner:

> *Salesperson: "Have you noticed how lightweight this jacket is?" (The salesperson places the jacket in the prospect's hands.)*

> *Prospect: "Yes, it is light. It's not much heavier than a shirt."*

> *Salesperson: "I'm also assuming that you want a jacket that is currently in style?"*

> *Prospect: "Yes. I do."*

> *Salesperson: "Well, this is the latest style which is currently being worn on campus. Have you seen it recently?"*

> *Prospect: "Yes, I saw several students wearing jackets like this at last week's football game."*

> *Salesperson: "We also realize that students have limited budgets and that price is very important to them. It was that way when I was in college and I'm sure it's that same today!"*

> *Prospect: "It sure is!"*

> *Salesperson: "Well, we have an introductory sale offer this week and most of our merchandise is reduced by 20 percent."*

> *Prospect: "Is there a reduced price on this jacket?"*

> *Salesperson: "Yes, but only for this week. Let's have you try it on to see how it fits."*

> *Prospect: "It fits perfect."*

> *Salesperson: "Yes, it does. It also looks good on you. Should I wrap this one up, or do you wish to look at some of the others.?"*

Prospect: *"No, this jacket is exactly what I've been looking for and I would like to charge it to my account."*

The above example is greatly condensed, and in actual practice the movement from one question to another would be slower and less direct. It should also be noted that a no answer can be equivalent to a yes answer, as illustrated in the buyer's last statement.

 **Indicate whether each of the following statements is true or false**

1. A salesperson should make as many points as possible before attempting to close the sale.
2. Salesperson should try to convince the prospect to buy the maximum number of items on the first call in case the prospect does not buy from her again.
3. A salesperson should be careful in using "the alternative-choice close" with all buyers.
4. It is often effective to have the prospect answer a series of minor questions with "yes" answers so she is predisposed to answer "yes" to a major request to buy.

Answer

1. False. Making all the points of a sale before closing is generally a poor practice because, if the close fails, the salesperson has nothing more to offer.
2. False. A salesperson's chances for a successful close and a favorable long-term relationship with the customer are increased if she sells only the specific number of items wanted and needed by the customer.
3. True. In using the "alternative-choice close," the salesperson must be reasonably certain that the prospect wishes to buy, or it will appear that the salesperson is trying high-pressure tactics.
4. True. A series of "yes" answers to minor questions develops a receptive attitude in the prospect which paves the way for a favorable response to the major question(s) in the close.

Summarize and review

It is good practice at the end of the presentation to summarize and review the major selling points of the product, particularly as they relate to the prospect's buying motives. Such a summary or review helps the prospect remember what had been covered and paves the way for the close. It also gives the salesperson an opportunity to determine if there are any additional questions that must be answered. In selling a tire it might be used in the following manner:

> *"The tire I have shown you has two tough fiber glass belts backed up by two nylon cord plies for inner strength, is guaranteed for 36 months rather than 12 or 24 months, is reduced in price by 20 percent, and we will allow you $5 on each of your old tires."*

Generally at the end of the summary the prospect will either indicate that she wishes to purchase the product or she will ask for additional information.

Get the prospect to make minor decisions first

The salesperson should get the prospect to agree on minor points before going on to major considerations. For example, in selling life insurance the salesperson might first get decisions as to the type of insurance the prospect wants and whom she would designate as her beneficiary. These are generally minor points which can be settled before proceeding to such major points as the fact amount of the policy and the monthly premium costs. This method is closely related to "assuming the sale is made" and "securing a series of acceptances." It differs by drawing a distinction between major and minor points.

The conditional method

In using this method, the salesperson offers to do something if the prospect agrees to buy. For example, in selling cattle feed the salesperson might say, "If I can show you that our feed will give you faster gain at a lower price, will you be interested in buying it?" This close can be used with buyers who have difficulty in deciding to buy. It should not be used, however, to cause a prospect to buy something which she does not want or need. Such selling would be high pressure and unethical. But if the prospect has a need for the product, and it will definitely benefit her, then the salesperson is justified in using this approach.

Pointing out greater risks of waiting

Sometimes the prospect will delay purchasing a product simply because she cannot make up her mind and thinks she has nothing to lose by waiting. In such cases, the salesperson can refer to higher costs or the creation of greater risks if the prospect waits. For example, in selling a file cabinet the salesperson might inform the customer of the fact that, within ten days the same cabinet will cost approximately $15 more because of the new labor and steel prices which will go into effect at the end of the month. Or in selling insulation the salesperson could say, "Next month will be much colder, and your heating bills will be even higher than they presently are. Furthermore, we now have time to do the work, but next month will be the peak of the season and we may not be able to schedule your job for several weeks." The salesperson must be sincere and truthful in using this method. She must also be reasonably certain of what will happen in the future rather than basing her statements on rumor or conjecture.

 ## Indicate whether each of the following statements is true or false

1. It is a good practice at the end of a sales presentation to summarize and review major selling points.
2. Agreement should normally be secured on minor sales points before proceeding to major or more critical points.
3. The conditional method of offering the prospect something if she agrees to buy should be used on those buyers who do not need the product.
4. If a prospect delays a purchase decision because she cannot make up her mind, it is a good idea to point out the possible cost of waiting.

Answer

1. True. A summary or review helps the prospect remember what has been covered and paves the way for the close.
2. True. Once agreement has been reached with the prospect on minor selling points, it is easier to get agreement on major points, which logically follow the initial agreements.
3. False. The conditional method can be used with buyers who have difficulty in deciding to buy, but it would be unethical to use such a technique on a buyer who does not need the good or service.
4. True. The technique of pointing out the cost of waiting should only be used when, in fact, costs are expected to rise and would adversely affect the prospect.

Limited supply

This method is used for products which are selling very rapidly and where the supply is limited. For example, the real estate salesperson may say, "You have indicated that this lot is ideal for your purposes, and inasmuch as it is the last piece of frontage on the lake, do you want me to reserve it for you now so you won't be disappointed?" Or in the case of selling ties, the salesperson says, "There are only three left, and we won't be able to reorder this particular style again." In this instance, the close is a combination of pointing out a limited supply and the possibility of incurring greater risk by waiting. Again, this method should not be used in a false or insincere manner.

Special offer or concession

Implementation of this method should be handled with care, for sometimes it gives the prospect the impression that she will get a better offer if she deliberately delays her purchase. Some companies promote the sale of their product by offering such inducements as a free accessory, a discount from the regular price if a certain quantity is purchased, an introductory offer, and so on. Giving the prospect something "extra" or "something for nothing" often serves as an effective tool in influencing her to buy.

Alteration of product

Sometimes the prospect will refrain from buying the product because it is not exactly what she wanted. She may object to buying a picture frame because it is the wrong color. In such a case it might be possible for the salesperson to repaint the frame in the color the prospect wishes. Or the prospect may wish to buy the same quantity, but because of convenience in handling she prefers it in several smaller containers rather than one large container. When the salesperson offers to alter the product to the prospect's personal specifications, it is difficult for the prospect to refuse the offer. However, the salesperson should always be certain the product can be altered, that the changes will be what the customer wants, and that the product can still be sold at a profit.

Trial offer

A trial offer can be highly effective in getting the prospect to buy. It is especially useful in those cases where the salesperson has done everything she possibly can and her only remaining alternative is to let the prospect use the product on a trial basis. The trial may be for a few days or a few weeks; and at the end of this period, the salesperson returns to attempt another close. The offer is particularly effective when there is no obligation on the part of the buyer, for it gives her a chance to determine for herself if the product will fulfill her needs. Sometimes the prospect fails to use the product. However, the salesperson can greatly minimize this problem by calling the prospect to determine if she has any questions in the use and operation of it.

Bringing in help for the close

Sometimes the salesperson needs assistance from another person to help close the sale. This is especially true for highly technical products or services. On the other hand, the second person may be able to explain something which the first salesperson missed. This approach must be used with care, for sometimes the prospect views the appearance of a second party as a means to "gang up" and pressure her.

Changing the course of the interview

Occasionally, after several closes have been attempted, it becomes necessary for the salesperson to switch gears. She must try another course. On doing so, she might suddenly stop talking about her product and switch the conversation to neutral ground. Or she may start to pack up her things and give the impression she is preparing to leave, thus reducing any tensions that may have developed and relaxing the prospect's buying defenses. Then, seeing the customer relaxed, she can casually refer to a point she failed to mention previously. If the prospect does not stop her, she will then enlarge on this point and eventually try another close. In using this method, the salesperson must not repeat herself and should be very careful not to exhaust the prospect's patience.

The direct appeal

This is a risky method for closing which should be used only as a last resort. In effect, rather than waiting for the customer to make up her mind, the salesperson does it for her. She asks directly for the order and might say something like this: "I have explained everything you wanted to know about the product. It is exactly what you need, and you know that it will save you money. You have followed my recommendations in the past and have never been disappointed. I assure you that you can do it again for I know you will be satisfied. If you have any additional questions or doubts, I'll be happy to clear them up. If not, then let's go ahead and I can have the installers here tomorrow." Successful use of this method is dependent upon excellent rapport with the prospect, knowing precisely what she needs and wants, and a record of satisfied service to build on. Also, the salesperson must be sincere and know that what she promises is certain to materialize.

Indicate whether each of the following statements is true or false

1. When a product is selling very rapidly, it is often effective to point out that supply is limited and the prospect should act now.
2. If a customer wants an item, but in slightly different form, an effective close is to offer to change the item to meet her expectations.
3. Hesitant prospects can often be sold by letting them use an item on a trial basis.
4. The direct appeal should be used in most cases

Answer

1. True. This technique is known as the "limited supply" method for closing and should only be used when it is true that the item is in short supply.
2. True. Slight alterations often spell the difference between success and failure in closing a sale. However, the salesperson should always be certain the changes can be made and at a profit for the firm.
3. True. A trial offer is particularly effective when there is no obligation on the part of the buyer, for it gives her a chance to determine for herself if the product will fulfill her needs.
4. False. The direct appeal is a risky method and should only be used as a last resort.

Special techniques for closing

The salesperson has a wide choice of methods to close the sale, and she will generally use them in combination rather than adhering to one single method. There are also a variety of techniques which will help to be more effective in closing. Some of the common ones are as follows:

Prevention of objection

An experienced salesperson will anticipate common objections that will be raised at the time of closing, and she will attempt to say or do something to prevent them from occurring. For example, if she determines that the prospect is a procrastinator, she might prevent this problem from occurring by saying, "Your problem is a serious one, and I know that you want to solve it as quickly as possible." The prospect generally will not disagree with such a statement, and at the same time the salesperson has taken steps to minimize subsequent procrastination. Another example could be, "I know on the basis of how you operate that quality is more important to you than price." Such a statement is designed to prevent or minimize the prospect's objecting to price later in the sale.

Narrowing the choice

Another effective technique is to narrow the choice. Sometimes the prospect wants the product, but she does not buy it because she cannot decide which style or model she wants. She often is in a state of complete confusion because she can't see the forest for the trees. For example, in selling a pair of shoes the salesperson will usually confuse the prospect if she shows her from 15 to 20 pairs of shoes. A more appropriate approach is to carefully determine the prospect's needs and preferences and to narrow her choice to two or three pairs.

Emphasizing key features

Some prospects may be interested in a product because it has a unique or different feature: the first car with an automatic transmission, the first self cleaning oven, an original figurine, the only lot on the street with a particular view, and so on. A special feature is of great importance to many prospects and may be the single factor which causes her to buy. If a prospect is so motivated, the salesperson should agree, compliment her on her choice, and emphasize how the product is uniquely different from all others.

Handling a third party

It is sometimes difficult to close a sale when another person appears on the scene. It may be a small child who interrupts by asking questions or detracting the parent's attention by crying or becoming unruly. The salesperson should be prepared for such incidents, which can occur in the prospect's home or in a business establishment. She might handle them by saying, "I have children of my own and know how tired they can get. If your mother doesn't object, I have a stick of sugarless gum that you might enjoy. And if you'll be good for a few more minutes, I just might give you another one." In other cases, the interrupting party may be an adult who asks questions which have already been covered; or worse, she criticizes the product. Such occurrences should not surprise or frustrate the salesperson. She should plan in advance how to handle them and be prepared for the unexpected.

Getting the signature or approval

When the time arrives for the prospect to sign for the product or service, she often becomes tense and nervous. The salesperson can help prepare her for this moment in the following ways:

- ▶ The salesperson can get the prospect to relax by having her sit down, or by offering her a cigarette, a cup of coffee, or a carbonated drink.
- ▶ The contract or order form should be brought out before the close. It can be referred to when discussing guarantees and warranties and should be a part of the presentation.
- ▶ The salesperson can get a pen in the prospect's hand prior to the close by having her calculate what her savings will be.
- ▶ The salesperson should handle the contract in a natural and relaxed manner.

▶ The prospect should be reassured that she is making a wise choice. If possible, the salesperson should offer to take the product back without charge if the prospect is not satisfied.

What to do if the prospect doesn't buy

It is a fact of life that the salesperson will usually make more presentations than sales. Depending upon the product or service being sold and the skill and experience of the salesperson, she may have to make two, three, or even more calls to get one sale. However, when closes fail, the salesperson must not become angry or argumentative with the prospect. Instead, she tries to retain and build good will. She thanks the prospect for the interview. She mentions that she will be in the area again at some future date and will be happy to call again. She leaves her card and other materials and encourages the prospect to call her if she can be of service. She might even give the prospect a small gift as a token of her appreciation for the time the prospect has spent with her. And she follows up by writing a brief note, mailing additional material, or telephoning. The salesperson should also attempt to analyze why her close failed and determine ways and means to prevent this from happening again. And most important of all, she should always remember that failure is more common than success, but success can be achieved through confidence and persistent effort.

❓ Indicate whether each of the following statements is true or false

1. An experienced salesperson will anticipate common objections and will attempt to prevent or forestall them.
2. A salesperson should always show a prospect her complete line of goods to assure that the prospect gets exactly what he wants.
3. If a salesperson fails to make a sale, she should follow up by writing a brief note, sending additional material, or making a brief phone call.
4. A salesperson should alter her methods significantly if after making a thorough presentation and overcoming all objections, a prospect does not buy.

Answer

1. True. By anticipating objections, a salesperson may offer a counter argument before the objection, since this effectively blocks the prospect from raising such objections.
2. False. A more appropriate approach is to carefully determine the prospect's needs and preferences and to narrow her choice to two or three items.

3. True. A salesperson should be friendly and helpful in all situations. A prospect who does not buy now may be quite receptive a month from now when her situation has changed.

4. False. In almost all areas of selling, the salesperson is more likely to lose the sale than gain it. Each presentation should be a learning device so that a salesperson can do better the next time. Some change in methods might be indicated, but not necessarily.

CHAPTER 12

Customer Relations

Today, selling takes place in a marketing-oriented economy in which the consumer is king. Successful selling is dependent upon repeat sales; and repeat sales ,in turn, depend upon having customers who are fully satisfied. The salesperson, then, not only must sell customers the first time, but also must do so in a manner that will create goodwill and a continuing relationship based on satisfaction of customer needs and wants.

How to develop good relations with customers

Serve rather than sell

The attitude that the salesperson has about customers will greatly determine how well she will serve them. She must practice the golden rule and treat them as she herself would want to be treated. In other words, she should sell as she would wish to be sold. In the long run, the salesperson's best interests and those of the customer are the same. By serving the customer to the best of her ability, the salesperson stands to gain.

Good customer relations begin by selling the customer a product or service which satisfies her. This means that the objective of the presentation is not solely making a sale in order to get a commission. More importantly, to continued success, is the ability to fulfill the customer's needs and to help solve her problems. The salesperson should fit the sale to the customer, even if it means selling less than the customer thinks she needs, or in some cases not selling to her at all. Such selling is based on complete honesty and a sincere desire to serve the buyer. If a customer knows that the salesperson operates in this manner, she will trust her and follow her recommendations. From this standpoint, then, good customer relations are developed by serving rather than selling.

Postsale instructions and helpful suggestions

Even if the customer is sold the appropriate product or service, she sometimes becomes dissatisfied because she used it in an incorrect manner. Therefore, after the sale has been made, the salesperson should make certain that the customer knows how to use and operate the product properly. She explains, demonstrates, and then has the customer go through the process to make certain she knows what she is doing. She also tells the customer to call her immediately if there is something she has forgotten or doesn't understand. And even if the customer doesn't contact her, the salesperson still should make a call to determine how everything is going. Such a follow-up minimizes problems that might occur and also demonstrates that the salesperson is genuinely concerned.

In addition, the salesperson should give the customer helpful suggestions that will increase her satisfaction in using the product. For example, after selling a battery, the salesperson might mention that the life of the battery will be prolonged by regularly checking its water level. Or after selling a knit suit, she can mention that care should be taken to avoid snagging on rough surfaces. Or in selling paint, she should give the customer a free mixing stick and also explain how to mix or thin the paint. Customers appreciate receiving such helpful hints, and they can greatly increase her satisfaction with the product or service.

Reassure the customer

The product the customer has purchased may be perfectly appropriate for her, but later she may begin to doubt the wisdom of her purchase. Such feelings can develop when payments commence on the product, or when someone else compares her product with the one the prospect has purchased. This is often a natural reaction--particularly after the newness of the product has worn off-- and the salesperson should take steps to prevent it from occurring. Consequently, at the end of the sale, she should reassure the customer that she has made a wise choice. She should also refer to later comparisons that might be made to competitive products and explain how the product she has purchased is superior to others.

 **Indicate whether each of the following statements is true or false**

1. A salesperson should always keep in mind that her primary objective is to "make the sale."
2. The salesperson's job is ended when the sale is made.
3. A salesperson can greatly enhance the value of a product to a buyer by explaining alternate uses, instructions for care, and so on.

4. Customers often have "second thoughts" about products and services and need to be reassured as to the wisdom of their choice.

Answer

1. False. The salesperson's primary objective should be to fulfill her customer's needs and to help solve her problems. She must accomplish this even if it means selling less than the customer thinks she needs or, in some cases, not selling her at all.
2. False. At the end of a sale, a salesperson should make certain that the customer knows how to properly use and operate the product. This process may last long after the sale is made.
3. True. Customers appreciate receiving helpful hints about the use and care of products and they can greatly increase her satisfaction with them.
4. True. Feelings of doubt often develop when payments start or when someone else compares her product with the one the customer has purchased. A salesperson must follow up her sales with reassurances that the customer has made a good decision.

Look for unrelated ways to help the customer

The salesperson will naturally want to give the customer helpful information related to the product or service purchased. However, she should also try to serve the customer in other ways if she possibly can. For example, if a customer mentions going on a trip and doesn't know the best route to take, the salesperson who recently made the same trip might be able to give her some helpful suggestions. Or if the customer comments about her failure to grow roses and the salesperson knows the cause of her problems, she should devote some time to telling her what to do. In offering such information the salesperson should:

- ▶ Be humble in her approach and avoid conveying the impression that she is an expert.
- ▶ Be careful not to embarrass the customer.
- ▶ Be certain that she knows what she is talking about.
- ▶ Avoid advising the customer to do something if there is a possibility that the outcome might be different than she promises.
- ▶ Refrain from offering unrelated advice or service as a means to obligate the customer.
- ▶ And she should not become so involved in referring to and doing other things that such activity interferes with her effectiveness as a salesperson. Her main job is to sell her product, and she should not let the tail wag the dog.

Express appreciation

Customers not only want to be served well, but they also want to be appreciated. Therefore, the salesperson should always thank the customer for her patronage. Expressions of appreciation need not be long and drawn out. Such statements as the following might be used:

> *"It has been a pleasure visiting with you, Mrs. Doe, and please call me if you have any further questions."*

> *"I appreciate your order, Mrs. Doe, and am looking forward to working with you."*

> *"I thank you for the time you have given me, Mrs. Doe, and greatly appreciate your patronage."*

Such statements should be warm and sincere, and it is appropriate for the salesperson to shake the customer's hand as she expresses them. A short follow-up letter is also an excellent gesture for expression appreciation.

Remember and recognize customers

Little acts of kindness are important in developing good customer relations. There are many instances where the salesperson can demonstrate that she genuinely cares for and takes an active interest in her customers. She can express these feelings in some of the following ways:

- Send the customer a card on her birthday, an anniversary date, and so on.
- Send the customer a card and/or gift if she or members of her family are ill or hospitalized.
- Write the customer a note of congratulations if she has been promoted, has received a special award, if her name has appeared in the news, and so on.
- Send the customer a Christmas card and/or a small gift as a token of appreciation for her patronage.

Customers appreciate being remembered and recognized and the salesperson should always be thoughtful about their problems and successes.

Develop a professional reputation

Customers must like and respect the salesperson if she is to gain their trust and confidence. Some of the ways she can build such a relationship is by keeping private information confidential. The customer should not be reluctant to talk honestly with the salesperson; and she in turn, should not be betray their confidence. She should also refrain from attacking or criticizing others. Speak well of someone or don't talk about her at all should generally be her motto. The salesperson who talks maliciously about others often conveys the impression that she talks about everyone (including the customer herself) in the same manner. In addition, it is most important for the salesperson to be truthful and honest. If delivery cannot be made when promised, then the salesperson should explain this to the buyer regardless of how disappointed she might be. There is no substitute for complete honesty, and the salesperson should always practice it. Finally, she should always be reliable, considerate, and courteous. A customer generally will not forsake a salesperson who treats her fairly and honestly.

Handle complaints properly

The first principle for handling complaints is to listen to what the customer has to say. Don't interrupt or contradict; instead thank her for bringing the problem to your attention and let her get it completely "off her chest." Second, ask or analyze what can be done to remedy the situation. Then, determine if the proposed solution or settlement is agreeable with the customer. And finally, follow through and make certain that what you promised is done. There is nothing more annoying than to find something wrong with the product and then not being able to have it corrected. Most customer complaints are justifiable, and ill feelings generally will be avoided if the salesperson is prompt and courteous in handling such matters.

Entertaining

The amount and kind of entertaining a salesperson does will vary with the type of selling in which she is engaged and the amount of money that is available for such purposes. In many types of selling, entertaining is not the custom; but in some situations it is expected, and customers may feel slighted if they are not entertained. The importance of the account and the time and money the salesperson has for entertaining should be the main factors for determining which customers and prospects should be entertained. Such entertaining should also be done in a spirit of sincere appreciation and friendliness rather than as a means to obligate the customer.

Holding accounts

Successful selling is continued selling to a satisfied customer. It begins by selling her the right product, at the right price, at the right time, and in the right amounts. It continues by calling on her regularly and by fulfilling her needs. The salesperson must not rest on her laurels and erroneously conclude that once the sale has been made, the buyer will automatically remain loyal and faithful to her. On the contrary, competition is extremely fierce, and customers will buy another product if they become dissatisfied with a certain product or service. Consequently, the salesperson must be constantly alert for any signals that might indicate that her customer is becoming dissatisfied or is beginning to drift away from her. Common signals to watch for are:

- A gradual or sudden drop in sales.
- Increased complaints about the product or service.
- More frequent reference to competitors' products and their respective advantages.
- Illness or inability of the customer to manage her business properly.
- Changes in the customer's business policies or personnel.
- Her being out of her office more than she should be when the salesperson calls, with the salesperson finding it increasingly more difficult to see her.
- Outside factors such as legislation, economic conditions, obsolescence, and so on, which can affect her continuance as a customer.

The salesperson should carefully watch for such changes and do everything she possibly can to correct or adjust to them. In those cases where she loses the account, she should determine why, how, when, and to whom the account was lost. The answers might help to prevent the problem from occurring with other customers and also give the salesperson some ideas for regaining the lost account.

 Indicate whether each of the following statements is true or false

1. A salesperson should end a presentation or sale by expressing appreciation for having had the opportunity to discuss her products or services.
2. It is usually a good practice to criticize other salespeople and products so that the customer does not look around for alternative choices.
3. Customer complaints should be listened to and handled promptly with little debate from the salesperson.
4. Once a salesperson has obtained a customer, she can be fairly certain that the customer will stay with her.

Answer

1. True. Statements of appreciation should be warm and sincere regardless of the outcome of the presentation. A short follow-up letter is also an excellent way of expressing appreciation.
2. False. A salesperson should always speak well of other people and products and be truthful and honest in her dealings. This will result in a feeling of trust and confidence from prospects and customers.
3. True. A salesperson should listen to complaints, determine what is equitable to both parties, propose a remedy and see if it is acceptable, and follow through to assure that action has been taken.

4. False. Competition is fierce for most products and services, and a customer will buy from someone else if she becomes dissatisfied with her present product or the service she is receiving.

As you can see in Table 12.1, there are many reasons that the selling process fails.

Table 12.1: Ten ways to lose a sale

1.	Not choosing prospects carefully
2.	Using evasive or deceptive prospecting techniques
3.	Talking too much and not asking questions
4.	Being insincere
5.	Focusing too much on the product and not on the customer
6.	Lacking standards
7.	Not being able to say or bear "no"
8.	Using too much convincing and persuading
9.	Lacking self-respect
10.	Creating an adversarial relationship

CHAPTER 13

Ethics in Selling

Ethics has to do with the moral principles governing conduct with what constitutes "good" actions and practices. What is "good" is generally evaluated according to some standard or code of ethics, either self-imposed or created by a society or some group within it, such as a profession or organization. Salespeople, too, have their personal and professional standards of conduct and we will discuss some aspects of ethics in selling in this chapter.

A major question debated by all concerned with ethical problems over the years has been that of absolute versus relative moral standards. Some believe that such things as absolutes-rules that apply always and under all circumstances--exist in moral conduct; others hold that only relative ethics are possible-that is, what is good necessarily varies with the time, the circumstances, and the situation.

Like most people living in a changing and imperfect world, the salesperson does not try to establish moral absolutes but rather strives to be as honest and professional as she can in the situation in which she finds herself. She recognizes that there are too many different types and levels of selling, too many complex sales situations, to always be able to say categorically that what is ethical and good in one will be applicable to all. Each sales situation must be studied to evaluate what will contribute to the good of all concerned, not just in the short run but also over a period of time. When situations are relatively simple and straightforward, it is easier to find the ethical solution. But in our highly competitive market economy, services and products to be sold have become increasingly complicated and technical. Because of the growing complexity of the environment in which selling takes place, the salesperson finds it ever more difficult, as well as more relevant and important, to practice ethical conduct.

To say that salespeople operate under a code of relative rather than absolute ethics is not to imply that ethics should be any less important in selling. On the contrary, because consumerism is a rising important force in the marketplace today, profit making can no longer be pursued by business to the exclusion of ethical and social consideration. Business must also be concerned with its social responsibilities to the consumer, to its workers, to the community, and to the nation as a whole. It is true that American business still operates in a competitive economy. However, the code of the social Darwinism, emphasizing survival of the fittest, is no longer acceptable.

Competition today must be tempered with a social conscience. Higher levels of education and improved methods of communication have contributed to making a person more aware of her social responsibilities. In addition, over half of our total population today is composed of people who are under 35 years of age. This predominantly younger group of consumers holds different ideas and tends to question past and existing practices. Ethics are, therefore, of increasing importance to the salesperson, and she should be fully informed as to how they relate to her particular activities.

The salesperson's responsibility to the consumer

The ethical salesperson will make it the major objective of her selling to serve and satisfy the consumer. In everyday practice this means that the salesperson should never sell the customer something she does not need. The product or service should be specifically geared to, and appropriate for, the customer; and if it will not benefit her, it is the salesperson's responsibility to so inform her. In other words, fulfilling the customer's needs or solving her problems is regarded as being of greater importance to the salesperson than the commission she can earn in making the sale.

To provide dedicated service to the consumer, the salesperson must keep informed on her product or service. Inadequate product knowledge can result in both ineffective and detrimental selling. In the case of a doctor, if she does not fully understand the effects of a drug, she can carelessly make a decision which could cause the death of her patient. In like fashion, the salesperson can harm the customer by giving her erroneous or inadequate information about the product and by failing to understand or by not caring about the customer's problems. Therefore, a salesperson that practices good ethics will refrain from making misleading, false, or uninformed statements about her product or service. She will also avoid using flattery, bribes, or high-pressure tactics to influence customers. Nor will she betray customer confidences or engage in personal gossip about her customers or others.

The salesperson's responsibility to her company

An ethical salesperson will also recognize her moral responsibilities to her company. Many salespeople have expense accounts and are easily tempted to "pad expenses." This practice, along with using company cars, equipment, and supplies for personal use, not only is dishonest but also greatly increases the costs of doing business. This ultimately can harm the salesperson herself as well as the company. The company also pays and relies on an individual to perform a given job. Consequently, if the salesperson works at less than her capacity, she is shortchanging her employer and simultaneously hurting herself in terms of personal growth and advancement.

Other unethical practices which are injurious to the company are faking customer reports, withholding vital information which the company needs, failure to use new tools or information provided by the company, and deliberately delaying sales until the company sponsors a contest. Sometimes an unscrupulous salesperson, in violation of company policy, will resort to lavish entertainment or the use of bribes to get business. Such practices have very damaging effects when less favored customers learn about them; and although the salesperson is the one at fault, her actions also create an unfavorable image for the company.

Some salespeople will occasionally have a second job on the side. There is nothing wrong with having extra outside employment as long as it does not interfere with one's major job.

However, it usually is very difficult to avoid "burning the candle at both ends," and the attention required by a second job will generally interfere with the salesperson's effectiveness in her principal one. Another related problem is for the salesperson to be involved in outside activities which represent a conflict of interest. Examples of this would be a salesperson who sells newspaper advertising and also serves on the board of directors of the local radio station, or a salesperson who sells plastic products and also has a financial interest in a wood product company. Generally, no person can serve two masters at the same time, and she is usually required to make a choice between the two.

Some companies make a practice of pirating sales people from other companies, particularly if the salesperson is employed by a company which is a leader in its field and has an excellent training program. The salesperson is free to seek different employment. However, when she is working for one employer, she should give that employer a full day's work and not betray her confidence. She should also give the company advance notice if she plans to accept another job, in order that her employer may have adequate time to find a replacement. In addition, all equipment and supplies belonging to the company should be returned, as should customer files, since they technically belong to the company and are needed by the person who will replace her.

? Indicate whether each of the following statements is true or false

1. Salespeople usually operate under a system of absolute ethics that are always applicable in any situation.

2. Salespeople must always remember that the sole purpose of operating a business is to make a profit for the owners.

3. A salesperson must occasionally make misleading, false, or uninformed statements about her products in order to make a sale.

4. A salesperson has ethical responsibilities to her prospects and customers but not to her company.

Answer

1. False. Sales people usually operate under a system of relative ethics, for it is virtually impossible to develop a single code of ethics that would cover all selling situations.
2. False. Profit is no longer the sole purpose of operating a business. Businesses must also be concerned with their social obligations to the consumer, to their workers, to the community, and to the nation as a whole.
3. False. An ethical salesperson will not refrain from making misleading, false, or uninformed statements, nor will he betray customer confidences.
4. False. A salesperson should be ethical about her expense account, her car and equipment, her sales reports, and all other relationships with her company.

The salesperson's responsibility to her competitors

It may appear strange that the salesperson has a responsibility to her competitors; one would think that the salesperson's only responsibility to those competing with her would be to outsell them. It is true that she will attempt to outsell her competitors. However, she must do it in an ethical and professional manner. In actual practice this means that the salesperson will emphasize the positive points of her own product or service rather than constantly "knocking" the competition. She will refrain from making misleading or false statements about the competitor's product, and also will not circulate any false rumors about its operations or salespeople. Such practices may give the salesperson a temporary advantage, but ultimately the truth will be known, and then the salesperson will usually lose the confidence of the customer and of others as well. In some instances some salespeople have been known to sabotage or damage competitor products in an attempt to increase their own sales. Needless to say, such actions are not only unethical but illegal as well, and any person who resorts to such desperate measures has no business selling. Resorting to such actions is usually caused by the salesperson's own insecurity and lack of ability, and such persons usually remain in selling for a very short period.

The salesperson's responsibility to her fellow salespeople

The salesperson also has a responsibility to her fellow salespeople. She should share information with them and be willing to help them out on certain problems. In the case of new or beginning salespeople, she should volunteer her services to help them learn their jobs. The salesperson is an individualist, but she must work together as members of a team. For if they work together and help each other the company will prosper and grow. If the company prospers and grows, the individual salesperson will prosper with it. Other ethical practices are to refrain from stealing sales from other salespeople and to avoid criticizing them in the presence of customers. The medical and legal professions are very strict in adhering to this standard, and salespeople should also practice it.

The salesperson's responsibility to the government and society

As previously discussed, business can no longer be regarded as an island unto itself with profit making as its sole objective. On the contrary, business activities today are recognized as being closely related with how we will live and the type of society we will live in. Our government has stepped in to protect the interests of society, and there are many laws affecting business practices. These laws, discussed in Chapter 6, relate not only to manufacturing of the product but such other aspects as pricing, discounts, allowances, advertising, warranties, and guarantees. The salesperson has a duty to be informed about these laws and to honor them. In addition, she should be concerned about the use of her product or service as it relates to society as a whole. She is not just an employee of a company, but also a member of the human race who should be as concerned as anyone else about such social problems as unemployment, pollution, crime, war, and poverty.

The salesperson owes something to herself and her family

Finally, the salesperson has a responsibility to herself and to her family. She should select selling work which is of real interest to her and commensurate with her abilities. Otherwise she may take out her frustrations and emotional upsets on her family and jeopardize her own health and happiness. If she likes her job and is good at it, she will not only help herself and her family but will make a greater contribution to society as a whole.

The salesperson has an obligation to keep herself in good physical and mental condition. Furthermore, she should keep herself challenged and motivated in order to avoid leveling off in a state of indifference and complacency as sometimes happens to seasoned salespeople who become content and cease striving to improve themselves.

Insofar as her family is concerned, she should remember that her effectiveness in selling greatly determines their social and economic status. What she does in selling will affect the care they will receive, where and the type of home they will live in, the comforts they will enjoy, and the degree of education they will receive. She is a provider in every respect, and her family relies and depends upon her.

In summary, ethics are the morals or principles we practice in doing our work. The basic philosophy underlying an acceptable code of ethics can best be expressed in these words: "Do unto others, as you would have others do unto you." Being ethical requires that the salesperson maintain a consideration of others, including her company, her fellow salespeople, competitors, society, and her family. In this way she will not only be an ethical salesperson, but a more successful one who has also helped to make a meaningful contribution to the world in which she lives.

? Indicate whether each of the following statements is true or false

1. A salesperson usually can gain a competitive edge over other salespeople by "knocking" the other person's goods and services.
2. In her efforts for promotion, a salesperson should avoid helping other salespeople because they might get the promotion instead.
3. The salesperson has a commitment to society and cannot separate herself from society's needs.
4. The salesperson's responsibility to her family is incompatible with her responsibility to her work.

Answer

1. False. "Knocking" the competition might give a salesperson a temporary advantage, but ultimately such a salesperson will lose the confidence of prospects and customers.
2. False. A salesperson is the member of a team, and by working together the team and the company will prosper and grow. A salesperson working alone cannot possibly accomplish what a cohesive corporate effort can do.
3. True. As a member of society, salespeople must be concerned with matters such as unemployment, pollution, crime, war, and poverty.
4. False. These two responsibilities are compatible. A salesperson should be happy with her work and work productively to assure her family a healthy and wholesome environment. Of course, it is possible to ignore the family or the work by devoting too much time to the other.

SMEI's International Code of Ethics for Sales and Marketing

Salesperson's of high standards in serving your company, its customers, and free enterprise

1. **I hereby acknowledge** my accountability to the organization for which I work and to society as a whole to improve sales knowledge and practice and to adhere to the highest professional standards in my work and personal relationships.

2. **My concept of selling** includes as its basic principle the sovereignty of all consumers in the marketplace and the necessity for mutual benefit to both buyer and seller in all transactions.

3. **I shall personally maintain** the highest standards of ethical and professional conduct in all my business relationships with customers, suppliers, colleagues, competitors, governmental agencies, and the public.

4. **I pledge to protect**, support, and promote the principles of consumer choice, competition, and innovation enterprise, consistent with relevant legislative public policy standards.

5. **I shall not knowingly participate** in actions, agreements, or marketing policies or practices which may be detrimental to customers, competitors, or established community social or economic policies or standards.

6. **I shall strive** to ensure that products and services are distributed through such channels and by such methods as will tend to optimize the distributive process by offering maximum customer value and service at minimum cost while providing fair and equitable compensation for all parties.

7. **I shall support efforts** to increase productivity or reduce costs of production or marketing through standardization or other methods, provided these methods do not stifle innovation or creativity.

8. **I believe prices** should reflect true value in use of the product or service to the customer, including the pricing of goods and services transferred among operating organizations worldwide.

9. **I acknowledge** that providing the best economic and social product value consistent with cost also includes: (a) recognizing the customer's right to expect safe products with clear instructions for their proper use and maintenance; (b) providing easily accessible channels for customer complaints; (c) investigating any customer dissatisfaction objectively and taking prompt and appropriate remedial action; (d) recognizing and supporting proven public policy objectives such as conserving energy and protecting the environment.

10.**I pledge my efforts** to assure that all marketing research, advertising, and presentations of products, services, or concepts are done clearly, truthfully, and in good taste so as not to mislead or offend customers. I further pledge to assure that all these activities are conducted in accordance with the highest standards of each profession and generally accepted principles of fair competition.

11.**I pledge to cooperate** fully in furthering the efforts of all institutions, media, professional associations, and other organizations to publicize this creed as widely as possible throughout the world.

CHAPTER 14

Personal Planning and Control

More than most occupations, selling permits a large measure of self-direction. Assuming that selling efforts must be planned and controlled -- and certainly success in selling can be achieved in no other way -- the salesperson cannot rely on others always to direct her work for her. Planning and control for the salesperson is largely a "do-it-yourself" activity. The self-directed salesperson is herself mainly responsible for determining what success she will achieve. Her internal motivations--her ambition and drive-- must be strong enough to keep her on the job and giving her best without external prodding. She must be capable of setting her own goals. She thinks clearly, plans, analyzes, and organizes her work. She has the necessary determination, persistence, and self-discipline to forge ahead regardless of obstacles. She is capable of adapting to changing circumstances, and she works constantly for self-improvement.

Establishing work goals

The salesperson will find it helpful to begin by forming a long-range plan as to what she wants to be and accomplish in life. She should have some idea what salary she plans to make next year, within 5 years, 10 years, and so on, until the time she retires. She should also have some idea of the position she hopes to have when she finally retires. Other considerations affecting the salesperson's goals and plans are the type of home she wishes to live in, how many children she will have, where she will send them to college, what she plans to do on vacations, where and when she plans to travel, and the possessions she eventually hopes to own.

It is true that one cannot expect life to go precisely as planned, for there are many uncontrollable variables, such as unavoidable illness, general economic conditions, unexpected misfortunes, and other unforeseen events which will greatly alter one's original plans. Yet, a self-directed person cannot completely resign herself to fate and blithely say, "Come what may." Such a person lets time, circumstances, and others manage her, rather than managing herself. To plan and manage your life means to have some goals and dreams of your own. It means that although you realize other factors can greatly change and modify your life, you still have some personal goals and purposes which motivate you to achieve and succeed. A salesperson's goals therefore determine her degree of motivation; and accordingly, her motivation greatly determines what she is and will become.

In addition to being "goal-oriented," the self-directed person will plan and organize for fulfilling her goals. In selling, this amounts to establishing personal sales quotas for the year, season, month, and in some cases, the week or day. Then these sales quotas must be related to types of products and the number of customers to whom he plans to sell.

Many salespeople evaluate their performance by computing a "performance index" figure which is arrived at by dividing actual sales by planned or expected sales.

For example, if the salesperson planned or expected her sales to be $10,000, $15,000, and $20,000 for the months of January, February, and March respectively, and her actual sales were $10,000, $13,500 and $22,500 for these three months; her performance index (P.I.) would be 100% for January, 90% for February, and 112 1/2 % for March. This calculation helps the salesperson to see how closely she achieved her monthly goals and also gives her some definite figures for determining what changes she will have to make if she intends to fulfill her expected volume for the entire year. It is much better to determine where you stand each week or month, when there is still time to make changes, rather than waiting until the end of the year, when it is too late to do anything about it. In other words, the "self-managed" salesperson will plan frequently and periodically rather than just once or twice a year.

In addition to annual and monthly sales volumes, the salesperson should analyze such other ***quantitative*** aspects as:

a) Sales volume breakdowns based on product lines; geographic areas or territories; types of customers; whether the sale is made by mail, telephone, or in person; cash or charge sales; and so on.

b) The number and average size of orders.

c) The average number of calls made to secure and service an order.

d) Amount of sales increase derived from selling more to existing accounts or from securing new accounts, and amount of sales decrease resulting from lost accounts.

Much of this information is provided by management and given to the salesperson on a periodic basis. It is important not to view the collection and analysis of such data as so-called "busy work." For the salesperson must first pinpoint her weaknesses and analyze their causes if she is to do an effective job of improving her performance.

If the salesperson plans to increase her business each year, she must sell more to existing accounts and also secure new accounts. Generally, there is greater opportunity for increasing sales by securing new accounts, for if the salesperson is doing an effective job with existing accounts, they ordinarily will be buying the maximum amount they can purchase from her. Consequently, she must devote a certain amount of time each week or month to securing new accounts. At the same time, she must continue to serve her existing customers adequately for if she fails to give them the attention they warrant, she may end up losing more accounts than she gains. It must also be remembered that the salesperson will automatically lose some customers each year. People move, retire, die, change jobs, or other situations occur which cause them to cancel accounts. It can be readily seen from these circumstances that the more successful a salesperson becomes, the busier she becomes. This is as it should be, for there is no easy shortcut to success; it is generally measured in terms of effort and work.

 ## Indicate whether each of the following statements is true or false

1. The self-managed salesperson must plan her work and work her plan.
2. A self-managed salesperson's goals should be solely based on the company's goals because the company is her source of compensation.
3. Sales quotas for salespeople should be established yearly because the company's quotas are usually yearly projections.
4. A salesperson may evaluate her performance by computing a "performance index" calculated by dividing actual sales by planned sales.
5. A salesperson achieves the greatest success by securing new accounts only.

Answer

1. True. A self-managed salesperson has goals and the desire to succeed, she knows how to plan and organize, she has determination, and she knows how to adapt to different situations.
2. False. A salesperson must establish goals for her life that takes into consideration her family, her personal satisfactions, and society as well as her employer.
3. False. A salesperson must establish quotas for each season, month, week, and day in order to maintain a "goal-oriented" life style. Yearly quotas are too broad to provide the incentive needed for day-to-day motivation.

4. True. The "performance index (P.I.)" is calculated by dividing actual sales by planned or expected sales. A salesperson should aim for a P.I. of 100 percent or better each month.

5. False. If a salesperson plans to increase her sales, she must sell more to existing accounts as well as securing new accounts.

Controlling selling time and energy

Considerable time is spent in preparing for a sale, traveling, and waiting to see prospects. The salesperson spends only about 20 percent of her time in face-to-face selling, and the remainder is devoted to other related activities. Consequently, time is money, and the salesperson must carefully plan and control it.

To make better use of her time the salesperson should analyze each of her customers in terms of their annual sales, miles traveled to reach them, number of visits per year, and other expenses connected with each account. In many sales organizations it is not uncommon to find that as few as 20 or 25 percent of the customers account for as much as 75 percent or 80 percent of the total sales volume. This does not mean that smaller accounts should be eliminated or ignored. On the contrary, the successful salesperson should and will have all sizes and types of accounts. However, she should allocate her time in proportion to the size and potential of the account.

Other means the salesperson can use to make better use of her time are to shorten her presentation and avoid needless repetition. Some salespeople say the same thing over and over again until they sound like a broken record. This is not selling, but a diffusion of meaningless words. Instead, the salesperson should carefully analyze the prospect's needs and concentrate on those points in making her presentation. It should always be remembered that an effective presentation is not judged by how many words are spoken, but rather by what is said and also how well it is said.

Idle talking or gossiping is another thief of time. It is very easy for the salesperson to become involved in conversations about something she is personally interested in particularly with congenial and likable customers. Such discussions can be about the salesperson's hobbies, her family, sports, the war, politics, or other situations which are of real interest to her. From time to time a certain amount of her conversations with customers will naturally be about these topics, for she should be well informed and interested in many things. However, she should guard against talking too much about such matters at the expense of her productivity in selling. She should always remember that she is a professional salesperson and her main job is to serve and sell.

Valuable time is also wasted by getting started late in the morning, taking unduly long coffee breaks, taking a long lunch, and quitting early. For example, on the basis of a 40 hour week, let us suppose that a salesperson starts at 8:45 a.m. rather than 8:00 a.m.; she takes two coffee breaks lasting a half hour each, rather than 15 minutes; she takes an hour and a half for lunch rather than one hour; she spends approximately 45 minutes each day in idle or needless conversation; then she spends approximately 45 minutes each day attending to personal business such as picking up groceries, shopping, and so on; and she quits at 4:15 p.m. rather than 5:00 p.m. Such a schedule results in approximately four lost hours each day, representing half of the salesperson's total (working) time. This is altogether too much lost time, and any salesperson that has habits like this should learn how to schedule herself more efficiently.

 ## Indicate whether each of the following statements is true or false

1. Salespeople spend most of their time in face-to-face selling.
2. Salespeople should concentrate their efforts on the major customers and not waste their time calling on small accounts.
3. Salespeople often get involved in idle conversations which waste their time as well as the customer's.
4. It is easy to lose half a day in seemingly harmless diversions that rob a salesperson of her productivity.

Answer

1. False. Only about 20 percent of a salesperson's time is spent in face-to-face selling; the remainder is spent on related activities such as travel, waiting, preparing reports, and so on.
2. False. The successful salesperson calls on all sizes of accounts, but she allocates her time in proportion to the potential of each account.
3. True. It is very easy for a salesperson to become involved in conversations about things she is interested in and such discussion are often helpful in establishing rapport with customers. But a salesperson must be very careful not to spend too much time on such matters.
4. True. A salesperson who starts 15 minutes late, takes two half-hour coffee breaks, an extra half-hour lunch break, and spends 45 minutes to do some chores and talk with the customer's employees, and quits at 4:15 rather than 5:00 P.M. may lose half of her productive time each day and not be aware of it.

Much time is also lost in finding excuses for not going out to sell on a particular day. Typical alibis for each of the months sometimes are as follows:

- ▶ January--Too soon after Christmas and people have no money.
- ▶ February--Too cold.
- ▶ March--Unpredictable weather. The roads are often muddy making it difficult to travel.

- ▶ April--Customers too busy with spring planting, cleaning, and repairing the ravages of winter.
- ▶ May--Too many customers afflicted with spring fever.
- ▶ June--Time for swimming, boating, fishing, and gala summer weddings.
- ▶ July--Too hot.
- ▶ August--Vacation time.
- ▶ September--Back to school time. Customers also too busy preparing for winter.
- ▶ October--Football games, hunting, and time to enjoy the fall season.
- ▶ November--Lots of sickness and colds because of colder weather.
- ▶ December--Customers too busy preparing for Christmas.

The salesperson who falls back on the excuse that people are busy will accomplish nothing, for they are always busy except when they are ill, asleep, or deceased. The productive salesperson, however, will have definite goals and will attempt to fulfill them regardless of the circumstances that might prevail.

The salesperson should also carefully check the amount of time she generally spends with each of her customers. In many cases, such an analysis will reveal that she has a tendency to concentrate on congenial customers and to avoid the difficult ones. It is only natural for a salesperson to gravitate toward more likable customers; however, in terms of effective utilization of time it is more important for her to consider the amount the customer buys or her future potential.

Another common weakness is to continue calling on accounts that will never buy. The saying that "If at first you don't succeed, then try again," should certainly be practiced, for in most instances it requires several calls before a sale can be made. However, each call should be carefully planned to bring the salesperson closer to the sale, and she should have a criteria for determining at what point she will discontinue her efforts. Moreover, such action should not be viewed as that of a "quitter." On the contrary, the salesperson's time is a valuable commodity, and she should not waste it on prospects who will never buy.

Much time is spent in traveling and waiting to see customers. Rather than listening to the car radio or reading a magazine in the waiting room, the salesperson can often use these times to learn more about her job. As she is driving, she can listen to tapes on selling which are played on small and inexpensive recording machines, or she can carry reading material with her which pertains to various aspects of selling and read it while she is waiting to see prospects. She can also do some of her report writing or record keeping while waiting. The reader should not conclude from this discussion that the salesperson should incessantly drive herself or keep herself busy every single minute of the day. Instead, she should work in a natural and relaxed manner, but at the same time be careful not to waste her time.

Daily plans

To avoid wasted calls and actions, the salesperson should carefully plan each day's work in advance. Following are the items she should consider:

a) Determine the persons who will be visited.

b) Consider where they are located and arranged the visits in a systematic order.

c) Review what had happened on previous visits.

d) Pinpoint the specific needs and problems of each customer or prospect.

e) Carefully determine what you plan to do, and the amount of time you will spend on each visit.

f) Gather and prepare materials specifically designed for each customer or prospect.

Careful planning in the beginning will minimize wasted time in the field. Selling is very comparable to flying a plane. Before the pilot takes off she must know where she is going, what bearing she will follow to reach her destination, how long it will take, at what speed she will travel, and prevailing weather conditions. She does not fly in a given direction and hope that she will eventually reach her destination. On the contrary, the whole flight is carefully planned and scheduled from its beginning to the very end. So it is with selling. Similarly, the salesperson must carefully plan her day's activities in advance if she is to utilize her time effectively. Lost sales can easily happen, but successful ones must be carefully organized and planned.

Controlling expenses

So far sales have been the main measure mentioned for increasing productivity. However, at the same time, expenses must also be analyzed and controlled, for they are directly related to earnings and profits. General considerations for reducing expenses are to:

1. Analyze the size of each account in relation to the expenses to service it. These expenses should include the number of calls made per year, distance traveled, telephone and mailing costs, and special services provided. Such an analysis will often reveal that a disproportionate amount of time and money is often spent on less productive accounts.

2. Reduce traveling expenses by planning in advance, routing in a systematic manner, making appointments, and using the telephone or mail to contact customers when possible.

3. Use advertising for increasing sales. It is usually an effective tool. However, the salesperson should carefully plan and schedule her use of advertising,

avoid needless duplication or repetition, and analyze its costs in relation to its objectives and/or sales generated.

4. Remember that written communications are less expensive and often more complete and accurate than telephone calls.

5. Eat well, but avoid luxury restaurants.

6. Stay in clean and comfortable hotels or motels and avoid the plush ones.

7. Be moderate in entertaining.

Management generally has explicit policies regarding these latter expenses. The salesperson should also recognize that the expenses of operating a business are progressively higher each year, and she should work with management in a cooperative manner to help control them.

? Indicate whether each of the following statements is true or false

1. Many salespeople unknowingly waste their time calling on accounts which have little extra potential or none at all.

2. Much of a salesperson's time is wasted in driving from customer to customer and waiting to see people, and there is nothing that she can do to make this time productive.

3. A salesperson should not bother planning her day's activities because too many unforeseen factors may affect what she does.

4. A salesperson has too many other more important duties than to bother with analyzing travel costs, expenses related to various accounts, and other such accounting problems.

Answer

1. True. Salespeople have a tendency to call on congenial accounts and to avoid difficult ones. They also tend to spend too much time on accounts that are not moving closer to a sale. Therefore, a salesperson must carefully evaluate each account to determine how much time she should spend with each.

2. False. Rather than listening to the car radio or reading a magazine in a waiting room, a salesperson could put this time to work by keeping records, preparing reports, listening to educational cassette tapes, and/or analyzing her last presentation.

3. False. Careful daily plans will minimize wasted time in the field. Proper scheduling can minimize driving distances, and planning her objectives for each account will minimize unnecessary talk and delays.

4. False. Expenses are as important to profits as are sales. A salesperson is responsible for determining, analyzing, and minimizing the costs associated with her job.

Record keeping

Every business firm has to keep records in order to schedule orders and inventories, to plan production, and to determine its financial position. There would be complete chaos without them. A similar need for record keeping also applies to the salesperson's activities, for records are an important tool for effective planning and utilization of her time.

Generally, two sets of records should be kept--one on current customers and another on prospects. The information to be recorded will vary with the type of product or service being sold. Items most frequently recorded are:

a) The customer's name, address, and telephone number.
b) The date of each visit.
c) The date, amount, and type of each sales.
d) The specific needs and problems of each customer or prospect.
e) Points emphasized by the salesperson on each visit.
f) Other miscellaneous points.

The above listing is only a suggested one, and many other items can be added. However, the important point is for the salesperson to keep some form of records. She makes hundreds of calls each year, and it is humanly impossible for her to remember everything that has happened. The increased use of new technological devices such as cell phones, notebook computers, and palms helps to record most of the information needed by the salesperson. There are a multitude of things to remember, and record keeping on a continuing basis is a necessary adjunct for efficient and successful selling. Salespeople also are frequently promoted from smaller to larger territories or to supervisory positions and should maintain records which will help the person who succeeds them.

Use of off-the-the job time

What the salesperson does outside her work is her own personal business. However, such activities will have a direct or indirect effect upon her work and she should evaluate them in terms of the extent to which they will help or hinder her in her performance as a salesperson. In this respect, two general recommendations can be made. First, the salesperson is not just a businessperson. She is also a member of a community and should take an active part in its activities. This means belonging to certain groups and organizations, such as the Parent Teachers Association, a local church, the Chamber of Commerce, Kiwanis, the Rotary Club, the local Citizen's Committee, and many others. It is her duty and responsibility as a parent and citizen to be active in such groups, for they help to improve our communities and nation. It is not necessary for her to belong to everything. Actually, it is better to participate actively in a few organizations than to belong to many in name only. In some cases, a salesperson can be involved in so many organizations that she is unable to devote adequate time to her work. Such a schedule should be avoided and she should limit herself to those organizations in which she can actively participate without interfering with her job. Such an arrangement not only allows her to make a contribution to her fellow person, but it can also help her to gain respect and stature in the community. The salesperson should belong to professional organizations which are related to her particular type of selling. These organizations keep her informed as to what is happening in her particular area of selling, and also provide her with valuable information for improving her performance.

The second recommendation is to take time out for leisure activities. Like almost all types of work, selling has certain pressures. It is important for the salesperson to periodically escape these tensions. She should set aside some time each week to pursue a hobby, see a play, watch a baseball or football game, go hunting or fishing, play golf, go boating or swimming, or engage in other similar forms of recreation. Rather than detracting from her work, these activities serve to rejuvenate and make her more productive on the job. There is no shortcut to success; it is generally measured in terms of the effort an individual expends. However, it is equally important for her to take time out to relax, reflect, and rejuvenate herself.

Subjective evaluation

In order to improve her performance the salesperson should also periodically evaluate herself on a subjective basis. This normally is done by using rating or self-evaluation forms which ask such questions as:

- Do I know enough about my product or service?
- Do I do an adequate job of preparing and organizing myself? What type of image do I project in terms of my appearance and personality?
- How effective is my approach?
- How effective am I in "sizing up" the customer and in determining her needs and problems?
- Do I generate self-confidence and enthusiasm?
- How effective am I in dramatizing my product and in proving selling points?

▶ How skillful am I in handling objections?

▶ Do I know how to recognize closing signals?

▶ How skillful am I in executing closes?

▶ Do I follow up after each sale to make certain the customer is completely satisfied?

▶ To what extent can I increase my productivity by better routing, shorter coffee breaks, and better record keeping?

▶ Do I consistently try to secure a given number of new accounts each week or month, and how successful am I in achieving these goals?

▶ Do I consistently try to improve my performance by reading articles on selling, taking courses, or attending sales meetings?

The above questions are typical of those that are commonly used in self-evaluation tests, and many more can be added. More complete evaluations can be obtained by having them made by other persons, such as the sales manager, the sales trainer, fellow salespeople, and customers. The important thing is that the salesperson cannot improve herself unless she analyzes her weaknesses and experiments with methods to correct them. A salesperson that wants to be a true professional will always try to evaluate herself regardless of how successful she is. She also knows that this is a never-ending process and that she must constantly search for new ideas and methods.

Maintain good health

The salesperson, in addition to being concerned about her productivity, should also do whatever she can to achieve and maintain good health. Good physical and mental conditions are important to any salesperson who wants to be effective in her work. In maintaining good health the salesperson should exercise regularly and watch her weight-particularly after 35 or 40 years of age, when a decrease in physical activity and a rich diet often lead to a gain in weight. The excess fat is put on at the expense of muscle and simultaneously puts a greater strain on the heart. A diet heavy in saturated fats along with insufficient exercise is often cited as the cause of cholesterol deposits in the blood which lead to arteriosclerosis and heart attacks. Therefore, the salesperson should exercise regularly and watch her diet so as to maintain a weight, which is appropriate for her particular age and height.

Taking time out to relax or vacation is also necessary for maintaining good health. Periodic relief from everyday tensions helps to restore the joy of living. It is equally important to get a proper amount of rest each night, the amount required varying with the individual. Some people can get by with 6 or 7 hours of sleep, others need 8, and some may require 9 or 10 or even more. In any case, if a person is to do a full day's work and is to be effective in what she is doing, she must be well rested and have the necessary energy to do it.

The "self-managed" salesperson will also have a physical checkup at regular intervals and will promptly respond to symptoms by seeking medical help. Some people foolishly delay attending to an ailment, thinking it is nothing serious and that it will eventually disappear. This might be true in some cases, but generally even minor ailments should be attended to promptly. "An ounce of prevention is worth a pound of cure," and your personal health is too valuable a commodity with which to gamble.

As discussed in Chapter 2, the salesperson should be optimistic and have the right mental attitude about her work and life in general. Her state of mind will have a definite effect upon her mental and physical condition. Happiness and the right mental attitude are vital ingredients for maintaining good health.

Finally, the salesperson should avoid smoking and excessive drinking. Current research has linked smoking with heart disease and lung cancer. As for drinking, it is an acceptable and enjoyable social custom but should be done in moderation. Nor should a person drink or use drugs to escape reality or to drown her troubles. This will only compound her problems and result in lost time, poor work performance, strained family relations, and deterioration of her health.

❓ Indicate whether each of the following statements is true or false

1. A salesperson should keep two sets of records--one for customers and another for prospects.
2. Salespeople should participate in community activities in their off-the-job time but should limit the time devoted to such activities.
3. Salespeople need not spend much time in self-analysis of their effectiveness because the company does it periodically for them.
4. Successful salespeople work hard day and night and take few breaks or vacations.

Answer

1. True. The information needed about customers and prospects normally includes: name, address, and phone number; dates of visits; amount and type of sale achieved, if any; problems, if any; points emphasized on call; and other miscellaneous items.
2. True. A salesperson is part of the community and should take an active part in its activities such as the P.T.A., Kiwanis, and her church. She should not participate to the extent that it prevents her from spending adequate time on her job or with her family.

3. False. In order to improve her performance, a salesperson should periodically review herself on a subjective basis to test her product knowledge, her image, her presentation, and her relationship with her clients.

4. False. Taking time out to relax or vacation is necessary for good health. A tired salesperson is not a sharp salesperson.

CHAPTER 15

Retail Selling

Retail selling differs from other types of selling mainly in that it takes place in a store to which the prospect comes. She often arrives with some preconceived ideas regarding what she wants, and she is usually closer to buying than are prospects when they are approached by the outside salesperson. The store name, advertising, special sales, eye-catching displays, and pleasant surroundings create a favorable environment that helps the salesperson to sell.

The retail salesperson generally sells in an atmosphere where there is less noise, fewer interruptions, and less time pressure. Also, in retail selling the salesperson generally handles more products than does a typical outside salesperson. In addition, the retail salesperson normally does not have the degree of freedom and independence that an outside salesperson has in terms of deciding when, where, how, and to whom she will sell. Another difference is that retail selling tends to place more emphasis on buying versus selling. Prospects usually expect more selling effort by an outside salesperson, but a retail salesperson must be more low keyed and may even deliberately avoid too much emphasis on selling. Her prospects have already made up their minds to a great extent, and they therefore tend to resist or resent too much emphasis on salesmanship per se.

Basic processes and purposes

The processes in retail selling normally follow these seven steps:

1. The customer is approached with a greeting or question.
2. The salesperson determines what the prospect needs or wants.
3. Merchandise is selected in accordance with the prospect's requests; then it is shown, explained, and demonstrated with its benefits emphasized.
4. Questions and objections are answered and handled.
5. A close is attempted, along with suggestion selling if it is appropriate.
6. The merchandise is wrapped, then payment is received or the merchandise is charged.
7. Last, the customer is assured that she has made a wise purchase, is thanked for her patronage, is given additional advice or free items, is invited to come

back again, and encouraged to contact the salesperson if there are any additional questions or problems.

The major purpose of the sale is to serve and satisfy the customer. The retail salesperson has also been trained to act as if the customer is always right and to accept the fact that the buyer should never be sold something she does not need. This objective is often expressed as "selling products that won't come back to customers who will."

Retail selling should also be distinguished from "clerking," where little or no selling is done. The clerk's duties simply are to show the prospect where the merchandise is located, to wrap it if she decides to buy, and to receive payment or make out a charge sale. Hence, there is a big difference between clerking and selling. Clerking is less involved and largely mechanical, whereas, selling is more complex and requires infinitely more skill.

Approaching the retail customer

The three types of openings which are generally used in retail selling are the greeting or comment approach, the service approach, and the merchandise approach.

The greeting or comment approach is often expressed in such words as:

"Good morning, afternoon, or evening."

"It certainly is a nice day, isn't it?"

"It was just announced that our local team won the district championship."

"It was just announced that the tornado alert has been lifted."

"How do you do, ma'am?"

The service approach is more direct and is used when saying:

"May I help you?"

"Are you being served?"

"Good afternoon, may I be of assistance?"

Service questions to avoid are:

"Are you looking for something?"

"Anything today?"

"Something for you today?"

"What'll you have?"

When the prospect is looking at or handling the merchandise, the salesperson can use a merchandise approach. It can be expressed by saying:

"That shirt is on special sale this week and has been marked down from $17.95 to $14.95."

"That sports coat is the one which we recently advertised."

"Those shoes were just received on a special shipment from England."

"That is the latest color which is featured in the new spring fashions."

"That paneling is the best we have. It is a half an inch thick."

"That tie is made of pure silk."

In using the merchandise approach, the salesperson should refer to major features of the product which she is reasonably certain will be of interest to the prospect. She should also mention only one or two points; otherwise the approach will be too long and may smack of high-pressure selling.

The manner in which the approach is made is more important than the particular approach itself. The customer should always be approached in a sincere and friendly manner. She looks upon herself as a guest who has been invited to the store and expects the salesperson to be pleased with her visit. The salesperson is therefore a host and should be polite and courteous when greeting her guests, the customers. It is especially important for the salesperson to remember this if she is doing something when the customer arrives.

In such cases, she may neglect the customer, or worse yet, appear annoyed. Idle gossiping or visiting with other salespeople in the presence of a customer is also bad. It costs money to attract customers to a store, and such behavior only drives them away. The salesperson should also be careful not to overdo the approach. It is appropriate to call a man "Sir," but inappropriate to address a woman as "Madam," which is altogether too affected. The salesperson should also avoid false flattery and "dripping honey" compliments. Instead, she should be sincere, friendly, businesslike, and polite.

Methods for increasing retail sales

The more important means for being productive in selling are to have the right attitude about selling, to know your merchandise, know how to analyze customer needs and wants, know how to organize the presentation, be skillful in persuading and closing, and know how to follow through and develop a customer following. However, sales can also be increased through suggestion selling, selling multiple or larger units, and "trading up."

Suggestion selling is selling additional merchandise which is related to the original purchase. For example, after selling a suit, the salesperson often suggests a shirt or tie to go with it. Or after selling a pair of shoes, it is often appropriate to suggest a par of socks, shoe polish, or extra laces. The suggested item normally should be lower in price and related to the original purchase. It is also good practice to display or show the related item with the original one during the presentation, rather than waiting to suggest it at the end of the first sale. In this way the second item often suggests itself without the salesperson having to mention it. In suggesting related items, the salesperson usually should not suggest more than one or two items because mentioning more than this number might be interpreted as high-pressure selling.

 Indicate whether each of the following statements is true or false

1. Retail salespeople place more emphasis on helping the customer to buy than selling the customer new ideas.
2. A retail salesperson is the same as a retail clerk.
3. The approach of a retail salesperson varies, but it must always be done in a sincere and friendly manner.
4. "Suggestion selling" will most likely be interpreted as high-pressure selling and is therefore not recommended.

Answer

1. True. A retail salesperson must be low-keyed and deliberately avoid too much emphasis on selling. Her prospects have already made up their minds to a great extent and tend to resist too much emphasis on salesmanship.
2. False. A clerk tells the prospect where merchandise is located, wraps desired merchandise, and receives payment. Retail selling is more complex and requires more skill in satisfying customer needs.
3. True. Retail salespeople may use the greeting, question, or merchandise approach, but the manner in which the approach is made is more important than the particular approach itself.

4. False. As long as only one or two items are suggested, this is an effective method of increasing sales. Suggestion selling is selling additional merchandise, which is related to the original purchase such as a tie with a suit. Often a suggestion of complementary items is gratefully received rather than interpreted as high-pressure selling.

Occasionally, unrelated items may be suggested to customers. There may be no relationship between a rake and a gallon of paint; but if the store is having an unusual close-out sale on paint at a bargain price, the salesperson might be doing the customer a service by mentioning it. For example, she might say something like this: "If you are interested in paint, our paint department is having a special close-out sale this week and offering it for one-half its original price." Chances are the customer will indicate she has no need for paint, but sometimes the unrelated item suggested may be something she is definitely interested in purchasing.

Sales may also be increased by selling more than one unit of the same product, or by selling it in larger amounts. For example, the salesperson might say, "These shrubs are $1.95 each or three for $5." Or the same ideas can be expressed by saying, "These shrubs are $1.95 each. However, if two are purchased, you may purchase a third one for one-half its regular price." Or in the case of selling milk, the salesperson can suggest buying more by saying, "Our milk is 35 cents a quart, 65 cents a half gallon, or $1.20 for a full gallon." Attempts to sell more than one unit or in larger quantities are especially appropriate for products which are frequently purchased or those which are commonly bought in lots of more than one. The salesperson should not look upon this type of selling as being high pressure, for in many cases the customer wishes to be informed about price differentials which can save her money.

Sales can also be increased by using **_alternative choice questions_** rather than asking the prospect if she wishes to make a single purchase. For example, it is better to say, "Do you wish to purchase one or two pairs?" rather than saying, "Do you wish to purchase a pair?" Another example would be, "May I fill it up, Sir?" rather than saying, "How many gallons do you wish to purchase, Sir?"

"Trading up" refers to suggesting that the customer buy a better-quality and higher-priced item than she originally intended to purchase. Great care should be exercised in using this type of suggestion because not all prospects can afford, nor do they need, the better and most costly merchandise.

An illustration of this would be the average homeowner who is interested in purchasing a circular saw. One has roller bearings and is priced at $49.95 and the other has ball bearings and is priced at $69.95. Actually, the $49.95 saw with roller bearings is satisfactory for her because she normally uses a saw no more than 10 or 12 times a year. Moreover, the total amount of cutting time usually is only two or three hours each time she uses it. On the other hand, the roller bearing saw priced at $79.95 is designed for heavy duty use. Professional carpenters and contractors need such a saw because they use it from two to four hours every day. Thus, the price level of the product should be geared to what the prospect needs as well as what she can afford. If the salesperson at the beginning of sale does not know the prospect's needs or what **she can afford**, it is usually advisable to start with the **middle** price, then go to the **higher** price if possible, and drop to the **lower** price if necessary.

It is also poor procedure to show the prospect too many products at once. To show her a great array of products may only confuse her and cause her to delay the purchase. Therefore, when the prospect indicates that she is not happy with one product, it should be removed so full attention can be devoted to the next product.

Know your merchandise

A major criticism frequently directed at the retail salesperson is that she does not know enough about her merchandise. Too often she is unable to answer basic questions about her product and her knowledge is limited to only knowing its different sizes or models and the difference prices of each. This is most unfortunate because customers expect the salesperson to know her merchandise and to be able to answer their questions. It is therefore important for her to know the **major selling points** of her product, the **benefits** it offers to the customer, and how it **compares** with other similar products.

For example, in selling a hardwood picture frame, she should have the information suggested in Figure 15.1.

Figure 15.1

Selling points	Benefits	Comparison
Made of selected hardwoods.	Atractive grain patterns.	Some frames are plain or covered with paper to look like hardwoods.
The corners are tightly stapled and glued.	A stronger frame will not come apart. Also there are no unsightly corner joints.	Some are just loosely nailed and come apart easily.
The edges of the frame are ridged and routed.	Makes it more attractive and decorative.	Some are just plain.

In selling a silk tie the points shown in Figure 15.2 should be mentioned.

Figure 15.2

Selling points	Benefits	Comparison
Made of pure silk.	Silk colors beautifully and has a rich, lustrous appearance. It also has a soft luxurious feel. (Have customer actually feel it.) Silk holds its knot. (This feature should also be demonstrated.)	Some ties are made of inexpensive rayon which has a harsher color and feel.
Yarn dyed	Each individual yarn is dyed, and the fabric therefore holds its colors better and is more uniformly colored.	Some colors are just printed on the finished fabric.

A hardwood picture frame and a silk tie are relatively simple, and products such as suits, appliances, and furniture, have many more features to which the salesperson can refer. For example, in selling a sports coat, reference can be made to the following points:

- The type of material it is made of and in what quantities.
- How it is woven.
- How it is dyed.
- How it is finished.
- The stitching on the collar and the lining underneath.
- The stitching on the lapel.
- The kind and number of buttons on the sleeves.
- The buttonholes, which are sewn with strong nylon.
- The two side pockets, which are stitched and fully lined inside with an extra built-in coin pocket.
- The stitched vents in back of the coat.
- The inside lining and the material of which it is made.

The salesperson who refers to such features distinguishes herself from the average salesperson and is able to give a more informative and convincing presentation. It is surprising how much valuable information can be obtained by reading the tags which are attached to the merchandise, asking the buyer and other salespeople questions regarding advertisements, and referring to product booklets and manuals. Effort and study on the salesperson's part to increase her knowledge of her stock will improve her performance and make her a more successful salesperson.

The store

In addition to knowing her merchandise, the salesperson needs to know certain things about the store. She should know something about its history, growth, and development; who its major officers are; what type of products and services the store carries, and where the various departments are located. She should also know the store's policies and procedures relating to delivery, credit, layaway sales, handling complaints, and making adjustments and refunds. Furthermore, she should know what items are being advertised, when, and in which media; as well as which items are marked down and on special display. How often have you gone into a store and asked a salesperson for information or instructions only to have her reply that she didn't know anything about it? Such a response makes the salesperson look foolish and also projects a poor image for the store. She should therefore be reasonably well informed about general store matters, and such information can easily be obtained from her immediate supervisor, the personnel office, company booklets and brochures, from other salespeople, and by reading the store's daily advertising.

 ## Indicate whether each of the following statements is true or false

1. Suggestion selling is limited to items which naturally are purchased with the primary selection.
2. It is always a good idea to trade up a prospect to a higher-priced item because the quality is usually better.
3. A retail salesperson should know more about a product than its major selling points.
4. A retail salesperson must be thoroughly familiar with the store, its policies, merchandise, and so on, in order to do an effective job.

Answer

1. False. If the store is having an unusual closeout sale on some unrelated item, the salesperson may be doing the customer a favor by mentioning it.
2. False. The price level of the product should be geared to what the prospect needs and can afford. Sometimes a lower-priced item is exactly what the customer should use.
3. True. It is important for a retail salesperson to know a product's major selling points, but she must also know the benefits it offers to the customer and how it compares with similar products.
4. True. A retail salesperson should know something about the store's history; its major officers; the kind of merchandise available; policies relating to credit, delivery, layaway, refunds, and other such services; and what items

are being advertised. Such information helps the salesperson to answer all of a customer's needs.

Substitution selling

The retail salesperson, more frequently than the outside salesperson, will find it necessary to suggest items other than the one requested by the customer--to practice substitution selling. In some cases, the store will not have the item which is requested by the customer; and in others it has the item requested, but the customer's choice may be inappropriate.

If the store **does not have** the item requested by the customer, the salesperson should immediately tell her so and refrain from criticizing the requested item or aggressively attempting to sell her something else. Instead, she should say something like this: "I'm sorry, but we don't carry that particular brand or product. However, I'll be happy to show you what we have." If the store has a product which is reasonably close to being what the customer wants, the salesperson should show it to the customer and put it in her hands for inspection. She should also emphasize its major selling points and refrain from referring to it as a substitute.

When the store **has the item** requested, but it may be inappropriate for the customer, the salesperson should follow these procedures. Show the customer the product requested and briefly mention its major selling points. Then show it alongside the more appropriate choice and also mention its selling points, but at greater length. Often a simple comparison will result in the customer deciding for herself that the suggested product is a more appropriate purchase. It is particularly important for the salesperson to be tactful lest she offend the customer. Under no circumstances should she say, "We have that product, but you really should consider something else." Even if the salesperson is right, customers will usually take offense to such a statement and may even leave the store.

Suggesting another more appropriate product is relatively common in selling gift items and other products which one party may be buying for another. If the selection appears to be inappropriate, it is the salesperson's responsibility to make an effort to switch the customer to a more suitable purchase. Generally, if an unwise purchase is made, the merchandise is either returned or the customer ultimately becomes dissatisfied and may never return to the store again.

Express appreciation and give the customer something

After a sale has been successfully made and the transaction has been handled, the salesperson should do five more things:

1. Assure her that she has made a wise purchase.

2. Actually give her something or give her some additional advice.

3. Thank the customer for her patronage.

4. Invite her to return again.

5. Tell her to call or come in if he has any further questions or problems.

For example, after selling a pair of shoes the salesperson might say something like this: "You're going to like those shoes, Mrs. Jones, because they'll wear like iron and you'll find them to be very comfortable. They might be a little tight to put on at first so I would like to give you this shoe horn. We greatly appreciate your business and please come back again. If you have any further questions or problems, don't hesitate to contact us. It's been a pleasure serving you, Mrs. Jones, and we'll see you again. Thank you."

Another example might be as follows in selling several gallons of paint: "You're going to enjoy working with this paint because it's so easy to apply. It will also outlast anything else on the market. Here are some sticks to stir it, and also a booklet with some helpful hints on painting. Thank you for your purchase, Mrs. Jones, and please come back again. If you have any further questions, don't hesitate to give us a call."

Sometimes customers will be undecided about the wisdom of their purchase. Or after they get home, they ask questions and begin to compare their product with others. Worse yet, sometimes other people will criticize the product which may cause the customer to become dissatisfied with her purchase. Consequently, she should be assured at the end of the sale that she has made a wise purchase and given some reasons to support this conclusion. Customers also want to be appreciated, so the salesperson should thank them for their business. When the salesperson offers additional help and gives her something after the sale is over, it shows that the salesperson is genuinely interested in serving the customer to the fullest extent. She not only sells the merchandise, but she also develops a pleased and satisfied customer who will return to purchase from her again.

Handling different types of customers

No two customers are the same. There are many ways to classify them, for example, according to age, sex, level of education, occupation, health, marital status, income, and religion. They will have different attitudes, habits, and personalities. All of these factors make selling extremely challenging. One of the main responsibilities of the salesperson is to analyze the type of person she is serving and to structure her presentation accordingly.

 ## Indicate whether each of the following statements is true or false

1. If a retail store is out of a particular item, the salesperson should disparage the item requested and suggest a substitute.
2. Even if the salesperson feels that an item requested by a customer is inappropriate, she should not try to switch her to something else.
3. Retail salespeople should always end the sale by assuring the customer that she made a wise purchase, thanking her for her patronage, and inviting her to return again and to call if she has any questions.
4. A retail salesperson must deal with a variety of people and must learn to evaluate the type of person she is serving and to structure her presentation accordingly.

Answer

1. False. A salesperson should not criticize an item that has been requested nor should she refer to a replacement item as a substitute. She should emphasize the positive points of her store's merchandise and demonstrate how it will solve the customer's needs.
2. False. It is a salesperson's responsibility to prevent a customer from making a wrong choice; otherwise, the customer will probably be dissatisfied and will want to return the merchandise.
3. True. Some customers are unsure about a purchase. A salesperson can minimize such worries by assuring the customer that the merchandise is appropriate by offering to answer any questions that may arise, and giving the customer the feeling that she welcomes her patronage.
4. True. Retail customers vary in age, sex, level of education, occupation, income, and other factors which make it necessary for the salesperson to adapt her presentation to the type of person she is serving.

Some of the common customer types, with suggestion for selling them, are described in the following paragraphs.

Just-looking type

This customer wants to look at the merchandise on her own and may start to leave if she is approached. Therefore, she should be left alone. The salesperson should also welcome her to look around and indicate that she will be nearby if the customer wishes assistance.

Hurried type

This customer is nervous and impatient; this indicates that she has little time or is in a hurry. Show her exactly what she is interested in, emphasize only a few major selling points, and be as brief as possible. Also, minimize interruptions, for she will often quickly leave if the salesperson momentarily attends to something else.

Uncertain type

This person is undecided, wavers from one product to another, and usually seeks answers to several questions from a companion or the salesperson. In handling this customer, the salesperson should be patient, watch for signs of interest to follow up on, and make appropriate suggestions. She should also avoid long lags or leaving the customer alone.

Confused type

This customer often buys merchandise about which she knows little or nothing. She may be old, a foreigner, or a child. This salesperson should put her at ease, be friendly and informal, determine her needs, and supply her with pertinent information in simple language. She should also refrain from asking too many questions for this may further confuse the customer.

Know-it-all type

The "know-it-all" is cocky, arrogant, makes a point of displaying her own knowledge about the merchandise, and frequently contradicts or questions salesperson's statements. The salesperson should attempt to disarm such a customer by being friendly and welcoming her comments. She should avoid arguing or disagreeing with the customer, try to utilize the customer's own comments to sell her, and offer to call the department manager for additional information.

Talkative type

This person enjoys talking about everything and anything. If left unchecked, she may leave without buying. The salesperson should be polite, listen for a few moments, and then refer back to the merchandise, thus maintaining control of the presentation. The salesperson should avoid being sidetracked and getting into a discussion of the customer's or her own personal affairs.

Quiet type

Occasionally there is a customer who says little or nothing, or she fails to respond to questions. The common procedures for handling her are to ask questions that can be answered with a "yes," get her involved by demonstrating and putting the merchandise in her hands, and repeat selling points in different words. The salesperson should not repeat herself in louder tones, implying that the customer can't hear, and also should avoid awkward pauses.

Easily distracted type

This person has something else on her mind or is easily distracted by an unruly child or outside noises. In handling her, the salesperson should attempt to eliminate the distraction if possible. She should also concentrate on the main selling points, be alert and peppy in order to maintain the customer's interest, and try to get her attention by asking questions and putting the merchandise in her hands.

Think-it-over type

This type of customer tends to put off buying decisions by saying she wants to "think it over." In handling this sort of person, the salesperson should avoid being high pressure, but at the same time she should ask questions and refer to major selling points, particularly those which are of key interest to the customer. Sometimes it is appropriate to ask her what additional points or questions she wishes to have explained. However, the salesperson should avoid doing this if she thinks it will give the impression of being high pressure.

Argumentative type

This person has a "chip on her shoulder," wants to argue, makes unreasonable demands, and refuses to be pleased. The salesperson should let her do most of the talking to "get it off her chest" and should be courteous, polite, cool and calm. She should tactfully ask questions and attempt to show how the product will fulfill the customer's needs or solve her problems.

 **Indicate whether each of the following statements is true or false**

1. A retail customer who is "just looking" should be given as much assistance as possible in order to help her find something he likes.
2. A retail customer who is in a hurry should be treated the same as all other customers in order to be fair.
3. The "know-it-all" type of customer should be deflated by arguing with her to show your superior knowledge.
4. If a customer wants to think it over, the salesperson should avoid being high pressure, but at the same time ask questions and refer to major selling points.

Answer

1. False. "Just-looking" customers want to look at merchandise on their own and often start to leave if approached. Therefore, they should be left alone.
2. False. A customer who is in a hurry should be shown exactly what she wants, only a few selling points should be mentioned, and interruptions should be minimized.
3. False. A salesperson should disarm "know-it-alls" by being friendly to them and welcoming their comments.
4. True. "Think-it-over" types should be asked questions and given major selling points, but not if this gives the impression of high pressure selling.

Handling more than one customer

Occasionally the salesperson will be required to handle more than one customer at a time. This creates a problem, because all the customers will want attention. The first customer, however, should receive priority. If the salesperson turns to a second customer and serves her, the first customer will feel neglected. On the other hand, the second customer or customers will not want to be kept waiting or to be totally ignored. In such cases the salesperson can say, "I'll be with you in a few moments..."

At times, especially if a second customer knows what she wants or has the merchandise in her hands and is waiting to pay for it, the salesperson can momentarily excuse herself from the first customer and promptly return to her after taking care of the second customer. It is also possible sometimes for the salesperson to give the second customer something to look at while she is serving the first customer. It may even be possible to serve several customers simultaneously, especially when selling such products as shoes, clothing, furniture, and similar products where the customer likes to look and closely examine the goods. In such instances the salesperson starts off with the first customer and gives her merchandise to examine. Then she proceeds to serve additional customers by doing the same thing with them, and returns to each of them throughout different phases of the sales process.

When a salesperson sells to a customer who is accompanied by another person--a husband, wife, son, daughter, or friend-- these persons should not be ignored by the salesperson. The recommended approach is to stay neutral or to determine which party has the stronger influence in deciding the purchase and to gear the presentation mainly to that person. However, in any case where there is disagreement among customers on what to buy, the salesperson should recommend the merchandise which she sincerely believes to be the appropriate choice.

Handling complaints

Customers will often return with complaints about the product resulting from improper use on their part or because of faulty merchandise. In either case, it is the salesperson's job to receive the complaint and to handle it in a manner that will satisfy the customer. The first thing she should do when approached by a dissatisfied customer is to thank her for bringing the matter to her attention. She lets the customer know that she cares and that the store stands behind its products. Next, the salesperson listens and determines the cause of the customer's grievance. She doesn't interrupt or correct her. She lets the dissatisfied customer tell the complete story and gets all the information relating to what happened, when, where, and under what circumstances. Then she either asks the customer what can be done to correct the problem, or mentions specific alternatives for solving it. And finally, she takes the necessary steps to correct the problem on the spot, or follows up within a few days with additional information or other means for solving it. She handles the matter as promptly as possible and follows through to make certain that what was promised is being done. There is nothing more annoying to a customer than to be told that her complaint will be attended to, and then for the salesperson to forget all about it. Such action is deplorable, and a salesperson should never make promises which she cannot or does not intend to fulfill.

Sometimes a problem is caused by another department in the store, and the salesperson is tempted to criticize that department in the presence of the customer. Such criticisms, however, should be avoided because they only result in projecting a poor image for the store. For example, if the problem was caused by late or slow delivery the salesperson should not say, "We're always having problems with our drivers, and they just can't remember when the merchandise is supposed to be delivered." Instead, she should say something like this: "Our drivers generally deliver on time, and I certainly will call this matter to their attention."

Usually the single most important cause for customer dissatisfaction stems from poor selling. Either the product was not right for the customer or the salesperson did a poor job in telling her how to use or operate it. Hence, a customer should never be sold a product she doesn't need, and the salesperson must also make certain that the buyer understands how to use it properly.

Handling returns

Sales returns can range from 5 to 15 percent or more of total sales volume. They reduce commissions and profits and are a common problem in retail selling. Some reasons why customers return goods are as follows:

a) An item may be defective in material or workmanship.

b) An item may be damaged or broken in delivery or returned because it was delivered too late.

c) Sometimes there is a mistake or misunderstanding regarding the quality and/or price of the merchandise.

d) High-pressure selling and letting the customer buy something which is not appropriate for her results in a high rate of returns.

e) A poorly informed or indifferent salesperson can also cause many returns.

f) Occasionally the customer will see something else which he prefers over the item she has purchased.

g) Sometimes goods are returned because unacceptable merchandise was substituted for what the customer ordered.

h) Frequently the customer will over order or request the wrong product.

Whatever the cause, it is the salesperson's responsibility to attempt to control and reduce returns. A high rate of returns hurts everyone, reflects unfavorably on the store, and results in lower profits. For the customer it is often embarrassing or annoying to return goods. And the salesperson loses, too, for handling returns can reduce her earnings and takes her away from serving other customers. In addition, it should be remembered that a *liberal* return policy can also help to increase sales, for customers will not be afraid to buy if they know they may return the goods. Generally, the store's largest credit customers do the most returning. Hence, if the store has a generous policy on accepting returned goods, the salesperson should emphasize this point. At the same time, it is her responsibility to do an effective job of selling so the goods will stay sold and not come back.

? Indicate whether each of the following statements is true or false

1. When faced with two or more customers, a retail salesperson always should wait on them in the order in which they arrive.

2. If a customer has friends or relatives with her, the salesperson should not ignore them in her presentation.

3. Customers with complaints should be handled in a direct and forceful manner, especially when the salesperson believes them to be wrong or unreasonable.

4. Policies on accepting returned goods could help to develop a positive store image as well as an unfavorable one.

Answer

1. False. The first customer should receive priority treatment, but sometimes other customers may be handled quickly and easily with little disruption.

Each case must be decided according to the circumstances that prevail.

2. True. The recommended approach for a group is to stay neutral and determine which party has the strongest influence in deciding the purchase and gear the presentation to her.

3. False. A customer with a complaint should be thanked for calling attention to the problem, her whole story should be carefully listened to, she should be asked what remedy she seeks, and steps should be taken to solve the problem promptly.

4. True. A liberal return policy may help to increase sales because customers will not be afraid to buy if they know they may return the goods. A strict return policy will often result in creating dissatisfied customers.

CHAPTER 16

Industrial Selling

Because of the unique nature of industrial products or services and basic differences in marketing and buying habits, industrial selling represents another major division of selling.

Classification of industrial products

Industrial products are classified into five basic categories:

1. *Major equipment or installations* including such items as production machines, lathes, presses, kilns, computers.
2. *Accessory equipment*, which generally is shorter lived and less expensive than major equipment or installations. Such equipment includes portable drills, electric lift trucks, typewriters, filing cases, wheelbarrows, and other similar products.
3. *Basic raw materials*, which are further, processed and converted into finished, physical products. Examples of basic raw materials would be cotton, sugar cane, cattle, wheat, tobacco, lumber, and iron ore.
4. *Component parts and materials*, which are similar to raw materials, but undergo further processing and generally are finished and ready for assembly. Examples of such products are automobile batteries, tires, small motors, wire, paper, and textiles.
5. *Supplies*, which are used in the daily operation of a company but are not fabricated into a final, finished product. Examples would be paint, light bulbs, cleaning solvents, lubricating oils and greases, pencils, paper clips, coal, and fuel oil.

Characteristics of industrial selling

Buyers of industrial products usually are technically trained and buy for business firms, institutions such as schools or hospitals, and governmental agencies. They are highly specialized and generally buy on a rational basis with their three major buying motives being quality, price, and service. In most cases, the product or service must be custom tailored to exacting company requirements. Consequently, the buyer's needs and problems must be carefully surveyed by the salesperson and specific selling programs should be prepared in advance of making the call.

Sales orders are generally of large size, are for a specified period of time, and usually are decided upon by several key persons such as the purchased agent, the chief engineer, the plant manager, the president, the director of marketing, and others. Negotiations for buying are often extended over long periods of time and are usually in accordance with predetermined specifications, which frequently involve competitive bidding.

Manufacturers of industrial products will generally have fewer salespeople than a manufacturer of consumer products. This occurs because industrial products are more selectively distributed versus consumer products, which are mass marketed.

The industrial salesperson will have fewer but larger accounts. Her presentations will be more technical, longer, and involve seeing several persons rather than one in the same company. She must, therefore, be skillful in adapting her presentation to several different persons.

Industrial selling is also supported by less advertising and promotional assistance than the selling of consumer goods for it is considerably more technical and requires more emphasis on personal selling versus general advertising. As a result of these differences, the industrial salesperson has more individual responsibility for selling. Because of geographical restrictions, the industrial salesperson is usually the only contact that the buyer has with the company she represents, and almost solely she determines its image. Such a relationship makes it necessary for the salesperson to know more abut company personnel and operating policies than is required of the salesperson that sells consumer goods. The industrial salesperson thus is more of a "consulting specialist" in comparison with other types of salespeople.

The channels of distribution in industrial markets are usually shorter, and selling is generally direct from the manufacturer to the user. Industrial demand is also a derived demand. What this market purchases is dependent upon what happens in end markets. For example, the amount of ore a steel mill buys is largely determined by the end market demand for automobiles, appliances, and other products made of steel.

Another characteristic of industrial selling is that occasionally reciprocity will be a factor in the sale. **Reciprocity** is the practice of buying from a particular company because it buys from you. If the product is comparable or better than competitive products in terms of quality, service, and price, such a practice poses no problem. As a matter of fact, under such circumstances it is the only logical, ethical, and sensible thing to do. However, problems occur when there is pressure to buy an inferior product reciprocally. Purchasing agents as a group, however, are professional and responsible persons, and generally they will not succumb to the pressures of undesirable reciprocity. Their job is to buy the best product at the lowest price, and in the majority of cases, this policy is followed.

It is also common practice from most companies to buy from more than one industrial salesperson. The risks are usually too great for a company to depend entirely on one supplier. Occasionally even the best of suppliers is unable to deliver the goods as promised because of such unforeseeable events as a strike, a plant breakdown, an unexpected inventory shortage, and other similar problems. Buying from two suppliers also has the added advantage of making the situation competitive and keeping both sellers "on their toes."

 ## Indicate whether each of the following statements is true or false

1. Industrial products are those, which become part of another product or are used in the manufacturing process.
2. Industrial buyers include institutions such as schools and hospitals, governmental agencies, and business firms.
3. Industrial buyers usually buy on the rational basis, and their major motives are quality, service, and price.
4. Most industrial buyers concentrate their purchases on one major supplier to get a better price.

Answer

1. True. Representative industrial products include heavy equipment, light equipment, raw materials, processed materials, and operating supplies.
2. True. Government agencies, business firms, and various institutions are classified as industrial buyers and usually place large orders, which are decided upon by several key people and negotiated over a long period of time. This sometimes involves predetermined specifications and competitive bidding.
3. True. Industrial buyers are highly specialized and generally have a technical background, so their decisions are usually based on rational motives such as quality, price, and service.
4. False. It is a common practice to buy from more than one company because the risks of potential strikes, breakdowns, or other problems are usually too great to depend on one supplier.

The industrial salesperson's requirements and qualifications

Industrial selling differs in several respects from other types of selling, especially where products are sold to middlepeople for resale or to ultimate consumers. One of the main differences is that the manufacturer of industrial products will generally have fewer salespeople than a manufacturer of consumer products. The industrial salesperson will also have fewer accounts. However, each of her calls will be more technical, longer, and involve seeing several persons rather than one in the same company in order to secure the sale. She is also supported by less advertising and promotional assistance than the salesperson of consumer goods. Consequently, the industrial salesperson has more individual responsibility for selling. Her success is greatly determined by her technical experience and her ability to precisely analyze the buyer's problems.

The industrial salesperson must be skillful in adapting her presentation to several highly qualified persons, such as purchasing agents, sales manager, accountants, the plant manager, the chief engineer, the president of the company, and several others. Moreover, because of geographical restrictions, she is usually the only contact that the buyer has with the company she represents, and almost solely she, therefore, determines its image. Such a relationship makes it necessary for her to know more about company personnel, operating policies, and services than is required of the salesperson that sells consumer goods. The industrial salesperson also serves more as a "consulting specialist" in comparison with other types of salespeople. Work in this area, therefore, requires a person who has technical expertise, good analytical abilities, and one who can creatively approach different problems in the field.

(?) Indicate whether each of the following statements is true or false

1. An industrial salesperson will usually have fewer accounts and her calls will be more technical, longer, and will involve seeing more decision makers than the typical salesperson of consumer products.
2. Because of geographical restrictions, an industrial salesperson is often the only contact between the company and the buyer.
3. An industrial salesperson serves as a "consulting specialist" to her customers.
4. An industrial salesperson usually deals only with purchasing agents and should plan her presentation accordingly.

Answer

1. True. The industrial salesperson has more individual responsibility for selling and she needs technical skills to call on fewer buyers with more complex problems.
2. True. An industrial salesperson often is the sole determinant of her company's image because she is the only contact the buyer has with the company.
3. True. As a consulting specialist, an industrial salesperson must have good analytical abilities and be able to creatively approach different problems in the geld.
4. False. An industrial salesperson must be skillful in understanding and adapting her presentation to sales managers, accountants, plant managers, chief engineers, company presidents, and others in addition to purchasing agents.

Industrial buying practices

The involvement of top management in buying decisions is quite common, particularly with large purchases and in smaller firms. The purchasing agent handles purchase orders and has considerable authority in the purchase of some items and less with others. For example, sales managers will often be involved in deciding on the quality of the product to be ordered, for its quality will influence the price to be charged and how successfully the finished product can be sold in the field.

Others are also often involved in the decision. For instance, in the case of selling steel, the industrial salesperson must work with and secure the approval of the designing engineers, the research department, the purchasing agent, production engineer, the sales manager, and others. Or in selling packaging material, she must clear the decision with the product planning department, the sales department, advertising, production, purchasing, the customer service department, shipping, and even the legal department. Hence, the industrial salesperson must understand many different operations within the company. She is usually selling to a "management team" with varying backgrounds and interest. She is also faced with the problem of constant changes that occur in the company. Frequently, people are promoted or transferred, titles and duties change, and it is not uncommon for fewer than 50 percent of those involved in buying decisions to remain in the same job throughout the year.

As mentioned, the major buying motives of the purchasing agent are quality, price, and service. Quality refers to the suitability of the product or service. It must fulfill specific requirements if it is to be successfully marketed. For example, steel must have a certain hardness to be used in tools. Consequently, a product not meeting the required degree of hardness would not be acceptable. This is why industrial buying is geared to predetermined specifications, and any product falling below requirements is automatically rejected. Quality can also refer to how the buyer regards the salesperson and the company she represents. Some salespeople and companies have a "quality" image while others do not.

Price is an important consideration in industrial selling, for the cost at which the material is bought will greatly influence the dollar volume of sales in the end market, as well as profits that will be made. The purchasing agent naturally attempts to purchase the best and most for the least amount of money. However, if the agent forces the seller to sell at an unprofitably price, it can often work against her own company's best interest. In such cases, the seller may be forced to "cut corners" by decreasing the quality or service she normally offers. Or she may simply stop selling to the purchasing agent and make it necessary for her to find a new source of supply. The old adage that "you get exactly what you pay for" certainly applies to industrial buying, and the purchasing agent must therefore weigh the importance of price in relation to the quality and service it buys.

Service includes such things as dependable and prompt delivery. It would be a problem of major proportions if a buying firm's entire production line had to be closed down because the seller had failed to deliver the material as promised. Service also includes prompt attention to problems or breakdowns that might occur after the product has been sold, research assistance and advice, and satisfactorily handling product returns and adjustments.

The purchasing agent is also concerned with the reactions and preferences of the employees who use the product or service that she buys. Brand A may be more effective and easier for them to use than brand B. Another factor she might consider is the company's objective of making their product more marketable by using a material or part, which is nationally advertised and has a high degree of consumer acceptance.

Purchasing agents are technically oriented and highly specialized in the products or services they buy. It is, therefore, easy to conclude that they buy strictly on the basis of reason and that emotions or subjective factors have little or no influence in their buying decisions. It is true that they apply specific and objective criteria in evaluating the products they buy. However, this does not mean that emotional factors are completely ruled out, particularly as prices become more competitive and product qualities become more similar. In such situations, company advertising and the personality of the salesperson become increasingly more important for determining which product will be purchased.

? Indicate whether each of the following statements is true or false

1. Top management is often involved in industrial buying decisions, and industrial salespeople must be able to make presentations to these top-level corporate officers.

2. An industrial salesperson often sells to a "management team" with varying backgrounds and interests, and she must adjust her presentation accordingly.
3. The only motive to buy for most purchasing agents is price.
4. Employee preference may be used as a selling point even if the product is higher priced.

Answer

1. True. Top management is often included in the decision-making process, as are sales managers and others in the firm.
2. True. When selling to management teams, a salesperson may face people she has never met before because of transfers, promotions, and so on. She must be able to adapt to these new people and vary her presentation accordingly.
3. False. Purchasing agents are concerned with quality and service as much as price and try to get the best and most, when they want it, at the lowest price.
4. True. Employees sometimes have definite preferences for products that are easier to use or are cleaner or safer. These are selling points, which overshadow price and service considerations.

Industrial sales presentations

The industrial salesperson generally does not attempt to sell a product or service on the first call. Instead, her objective usually is to get permission to make a survey of the buyer's operation. If the buyer agrees, the salesperson will often have additional personnel from the home office help in conducting the survey. This practice is especially common if the product is highly technical and involves several areas of specialization. The salesperson will also work closely with personnel of the buying company. When the survey is finished, the salesperson will prepare a formal report and present it to the purchasing agent and other interested parties. Many times it is presented to a group of people who serve as a formal buying committee.

In order to do an effective job, the industrial salesperson must carefully prepare her presentation prior to giving it. She must know all phases of the buyer's operation, the needs and interests of all the persons to whom she will be talking, and how she proposes to decrease their costs and thus increase their profits by using her product. This is no simple task and it requires extensive preparation. All the benefits she mentions must be supported with specific facts, figures, charts, graphs, and other materials. She will often use samples, models, sketches, slides, films, and other aids to illustrate her points. She must be "razor sharp" during the presentation and be able to field questions from everyone. All can be lost if she becomes confused or is unable to answer key questions.

In addition, the salesperson must gear her presentation to the specific interests of each person present, and at the same time make it of interest for the group as a whole. She should always identify the person who has the most authority in the group and attempt to involve her in the presentation in order to help influence the others. Sometimes, however, the leader of the group may remain silent during the presentation. Then the salesperson must involve those with less authority in such a manner as to convince the leader. In making her presentation, the salesperson will often use other persons from her company to help explain certain points which require a high degree of expertise. Frequently, she will also be accompanied by members of top management, including the CEO and vice president, particularly if the sale might result in an unusually large order.

To be a successful industrial salesperson requires considerable skill and training. Purchasing agents not only buy from her, but they also rely on her for information on new products, improvements, and new applications or uses. She also is a source of information on what other companies are doing. Purchasing agents expect the industrial salesperson to help them with their problems. They do not want her to take up their valuable time with idle conversation or unnecessary visits. Therefore, she must carefully plan each call and design it to serve the buyer in some specific way.

In summary, the work of an industrial salesperson is highly creative and challenging. It is also very rewarding work in terms of what is accomplished, the type of people with whom she works, and the money she earns.

Indicate whether each of the following statements is true or false

1. Usually, the purpose of an industrial salesperson's first call is to make a sales presentation.
2. It is a good idea to identify the person in the group who has the most authority and attempt to involve her in the sales presentation.
3. An industrial salesperson will often bring other members of her firm to a sales presentation to give her expert support.
4. Most firms view industrial salespeople as helpful consultants and problem solvers rather than as representatives of a particular firm or interest.

Answer

1. False. The industrial salesperson generally does not attempt to make a sale on her first call. Instead, her objective usually is to make a survey of the company's operation to determine what the buyers needs are.

2. True. This can have a great positive influence on others attending the meeting.

3. True. In making her presentation, an industrial salesperson will often call upon experts from her firm, including the CEO and vice president.

4. True. An industrial salesperson is often viewed as a consultant who is a source of information about what other companies are doing, new product developments, new applications of old products, and various problem-solving ideas. As such, she is a valuable help to the customer.

CHAPTER 17

Sales Management

Traditionally, sales management has been viewed as the management of such sales-related activities as recruiting and selecting a sales force and then training, evaluating, compensating, supervising, and motivating these salespeople. However, the responsibilities of the sales manager have been greatly expanded in many instances to include such related activities as product planning, pricing, sales forecasting, customer service, channel considerations, and advertising. As more and more firms become "marketing oriented" and with the increasing growth of consumerism, the sales manager of today is becoming more involved in the whole spectrum of marketing activities. Accordingly, her work is more complex and requires a higher degree of education and training.

Differences between sales management and other types of human resource management (HRM)

Though related to human resource management (HRM), sales management warrants special attention in comparison with the management of other classes of business human resources (such as accountants, office workers, and those in finance) because the salesperson's job is so different from other jobs within the company. This difference exists primarily because the salesperson is in the public eye more than other types of workers. The impressions that consumers have of a particular company and its products are often formed by their contact with the salesperson. Thus the salesperson is an official representative of the firm. Her work also differs from that of other workers in that she operates with a higher degree of freedom and independence; she has a great deal more freedom to determine her own productivity. In comparison with many other activities, the salesperson's work requires self-initiative, creativity, and persistence; and these qualities, in turn, require a higher degree of motivation.

The very nature of her work requires that the salesperson possess more social poise. In many instances she will be selling to persons who have high social or corporate standing, and she must be able to identify with, and be accepted by, these people. Such acceptance requires a high degree of social intelligence not ordinarily required in other types of work.

In addition, the salesperson is one of the few employees who is allowed to spend company funds. She is responsible for the amounts she will spend on travel, meals, lodging, and entertainment; and the expenses she incurs in these areas will greatly influence company costs and profits.

Finally, many selling jobs require considerable traveling and being away from home. Such circumstances, plus the fact that she will usually encounter a great deal of customer resistance, creates tensions and pressures that are absent in many other jobs. Because of these different circumstances and responsibilities, sales management demands special attention over and above that which management devotes to other types of business personnel.

Major responsibilities of the sales manager

The responsibilities of the sales manager will vary with the size and type of company, as well as with its corporate structure. Usually, however, her main responsibilities will be to supervise the sales force; to recruit, select, and train sales personnel; to manage the local sales office; to serve as the coordinating link between top management and the sales force; and in some cases, to engage in personal selling. Also, to the degree that her company accepts the marketing concept, she will be involved in decisions related to product development, pricing, the "marketing mix," and others.

In supervising the sales force, the sales manager assigns sales territories, determines quotas, and decides how the salespeople will be compensated. She is also concerned about how the salesperson allocates her time by types of customers and product lines. She attempts to secure maximum effectiveness by analyzing sales reports and suggesting work patterns. She must know how to motivate the salesperson by utilizing various incentives and rewards. This is a persistent problem because salespeople usually work alone in the field and can easily become discouraged. These conditions make motivation a major responsibility of the sales manager for the salesperson must continue to have a positive and determined attitude if she is to succeed. The sales manager must also evaluate the salesperson's performance--usually by comparing her actual sales with a predetermined or expected standard. In those cases where the salesperson's performance is unsatisfactory, the sales manager must know how to analyze the salesperson's problems and be able to make suggestions to help her.

In the recruiting, selection, and training of sales personnel, the sales manager is often aided by other persons. However, her policies will determine where and how persons will be selected, the methods that will be used in selecting them, and the type of program that will be developed to train them.

The sales manager's duties in managing the local office will vary greatly depending upon its size and functions. It may be operated by a single secretary, or in other cases by several secretaries, a bookkeeper or accountant, a service person, a janitor, a plant manager and her staff, a warehouseperson, and other similar personnel. The sales manager alone will be responsible for managing the operation of a smaller office; but for a larger one, she usually will have to employ an assistant sales manager and maybe even an office manager. As manager of the local sales office, she is also frequently responsible for representing the company. In this role she is expected to participate in local community affairs, to contribute to charities, and to participate in various service organizations.

In her role as the coordinating link between top management and the sales force, the sales manager must serve as an intermediary. It is her job to communicate the policies of top management to the salespeople; and in like fashion, to communicate the needs and problems of the salespeople to top management. This is no simple task because she is often caught between two conflicting viewpoints. For example, top management is always interested in controlling and reducing expenses, while salespeople sometimes are more interested in increasing sales with less concern about the expenses involved in achieving them. Nevertheless, the sales manager must know how to secure the cooperation of both groups, for it is her responsibility to get the job done.

 Indicate whether each of the following statements is true or false

1. Since around 1990's, the sales manager's responsibilities have been expanded in many companies to include product planning, pricing, customer service, channel considerations, and advertising.
2. The sales manager's job is no different from the management of other functional areas such as personnel, accounting, and finance.
3. One of the major responsibilities of the sales manager is to continually motivate the salespeople under her.
4. The duties of all sales managers are restricted to recruiting, selecting, and training sales personnel.

Answer

1. True. As more firms become marketing oriented, sales managers become more involved in the whole spectrum of marketing activities.

2. False. Since salespeople are in the public eye, directly spend corporate funds, work with a relative degree of independence and self-motivation, and travel extensively, the job of managing them is much different from that of managing other workers.

3. True. A sales manager must know how to motivate salespeople by utilizing various incentives and rewards. Motivation is a major responsibility, because salespeople must continue to have positive and determined attitudes if they are to succeed.

4. False. Sales managers have many duties besides recruiting, selecting, and training such as managing the local sales office, coordinating top management and sales efforts, personal selling to select accounts, and managing activities such as territory allocation, quotas, compensation, and time allocation.

Should the sales manager also sell?

Whether or not the sales manager should also do personal selling is one of the most controversial questions concerning her responsibilities. Arguments in favor of her selling are that major accounts usually require the attention of senior personnel, such as a sales manager. It is also argued that it is logical for her to continue to handle the major accounts she served as a salesperson. Furthermore, it is said that a sales manager cannot keep abreast of current problems in selling unless she herself continues to sell. Arguments against her selling are that it often puts her in competition with the salespeople under her while she has the advantage of picking the better accounts. Others contend that sales management and selling are two distinct functions, that each is a full-time job in itself, and that the two jobs should, therefore, be separated.

A key factor in these conflicting viewpoints is the fact that often the top salespeople are chosen for sales management positions. It cannot be disputed that demonstrated effectiveness in selling is an important asset for a sales manager. However, it does not guarantee that she will be a good manager. As a matter of fact, such traits as aggressiveness and the desire to be independent, which are usually associated with successful selling, might turn out to be detrimental traits when applied to managing others.

In summary, many successful salespeople can become successful sales managers, but sales management requires the ability to plan and organize and to work with and through others. Studies also show that successful sales managers receive higher salaries as compared with persons in other types of work. Annual sales of a firm are commonly regarded as a measure of its success. In this sense, the sales manager has considerable visibility and is one of the most important persons in the company. Consequently, successful selling experience and work as a sales manager are two of the fastest steps to higher corporate positions.

Sales forecasting

The sales manager is usually responsible for making company sales forecasts, which are an estimate of the sales that will be made for a particular period of time, such as a season or a year. The sales forecast is one of the key factors in arriving at the overall company budget. It becomes the blueprint for company planning, and the productive requirements of all the other departments are carefully geared to it. Sales managers who make short-run forecasts are interested in seasonal matters or developments; those making long-run forecasts are interested in trends.

There are several different approaches to forecasting company sales. Representative methods are discussed in the following paragraphs.

Management consensus

A consensus of opinions of top company executives as to what sales will be provides a quick and easy method of forecasting. Such a forecast will be based on inputs from several sources rather than a single source. But forecasts arrived at by this method sometimes amount to nothing more than educated guesses. Many of the persons who participate in making the forecast may be poorly qualified. Also, the data relating to the market on which executives base their predictions may be highly inaccurate. Moreover, it is often difficult to break this type of forecast down into quotas.

Sales force summary

A forecast may be arrived at by using estimates secured first from the salespeople and then carried upward through the sales organization, each level accumulating data from the preceding one and passing on a forecast based on inputs from the salespeople, then the regional and divisional managers make their estimates, and so the forecast moves upward to the highest marketing executive. Proponents of this method hold that the person who knows the market best is the salesperson herself, the person who is in closest contact with the consumer. The procedure is more realistic than depending solely on the views at the top, because the persons participating in the forecast are also the ones to who the quotas will be assigned. In addition, the weaknesses and dangers of one-person forecasts are avoided, and operating breakdowns of the forecast are relatively easy to make. Arguments against this method are that some salespeople will be too optimistic in their expectations, while others will be too pessimistic. It is argued that some will deliberately underestimate the market in order to get a smaller quota. Moreover, this method is quite time consuming, and some of the salespeople may resent having to participate. Finally, most salespeople are well informed about market conditions in their territories, but they may be poorly informed about economic conditions on a national level, which could affect company sales.

User estimates

Some companies will make their forecast by asking their customers what and how much they plan to buy for a given period. Advantages of this method are that the forecast is based on the estimates provided by the users whose buying actions will actually determine sales. It also gives the company a more detailed and better understanding of the buyers' intentions. Arguments against this method are that it is difficult to employ in markets where there are many customers or in markets where they may be difficult to locate. Such a forecast assumes that the product user will be well informed and willing to participate. However, in actual practice some of the product users will be poorly informed and indifferent or reluctant about participating. This method also bases the forecast on estimates, which are subject to possible change. Finally, it requires considerable time and manpower to collect such information.

Using past and current sales as basis for prediction

This method recognizes that past sales and current sales can help to predict what the future sales will be. For example, the forecaster may expect favorable changes again next year which will increase sales volume by approximately 10 percent as compared with an increase of 9 percent for the current year and an increase of 8 percent in the past year. Relatively simple and easy to use, this method can help predict both for the short term and the long term. However, putting so much emphasis on past and current sales may prevent recognition of changes in conditions that can occur quickly.

Taking account of changing economic and social conditions

In companies where sufficient economic and statistical expertise is available, the sales forecast can be made to reflect those changing conditions in the overall economy or in the industry, which could have an effect on the sales of the individual firm. Gross domestic product (GDP) and extension of future trends can be used as a measure of the present and expected business prosperity. The sales forecaster must then interpret the effect the anticipated upsurge or recession will have on her firm's sales.

Changing patterns in population, too, can be, taken into account. For example, when birthrate census data reveals a decline in the number of grade-school children in the population, this will serve to warn manufactures of products, designed for this age group to anticipate lower sales volume unless they can make up for the loss by increasing their market share.

Social patterns also must be watched for major changes in attitudes and tastes. When social attitudes discourage "keeping up with the Joneses," certain prestige products may suffer a loss in sales. A general shift away from materialistic values by the young would certainly have to be taken into account by those selling to the youth market. Sales forecasting is an important function and determines the budgeting for all operations of the firm. Several methods are used depending upon the size of the company, the type of product or service it sells, and the number of customers involved. Each method has its respective advantages and disadvantages, and the specific methods chosen to make a forecast are one of the major responsibilities of the sales manager.

? Indicate whether each of the following statements is true or false

1. One of the most controversial areas in sales management is whether or not the manager should be involved in personal selling.
2. The best salespeople always make the best managers.
3. Successful selling and work as a sales manager are two of the fastest steps to higher corporate positions.
4. Salespeople may or may not have a role in forecasting future sales.
5. Sales forecasts based on user's expectations or past sales have short-comings which limit their effectiveness.

Answer

1. True. There are arguments for and against using managers as field salespeople, but it is difficult to be a good manager and a good salesperson at the same time.
2. False. Demonstrated effectiveness in selling is an important asset for sales managers, but such traits as aggressiveness and a desire for independence, which are usually associated with successful selling, may be detrimental for managers.
3. True. The unique nature of sales management work makes it easier to evaluate performance and it is the only function, which generates profits for the company.
4. True. Salespeople are often too optimistic or pessimistic in their expectations, but they often know more than managers about the marketplace. Managers are often more expert in analyzing sales trends. Therefore, salespeople are often used in sales forecasting, but sometimes this is the sole responsibility of management.

5. True. User's expectations and past sales both are based on data, which may or may not be accurate in predicting future potential. Each forecasting method has its advantages and disadvantages, and choosing a method or combination of methods is a major responsibility of the sales manager.

Sales quotas

Sales quotas are amounts in dollars or units that the salesperson is expected to sell in a given territory for a given period of time. There are quotas for the salesperson; for each area or territory; for product lines; for buyers; and quotas for a month, season, or year.

Quotas are very important in selling, for without them there can be no effective planning and control. They set up targets or goals for the salesperson and her compensation, commissions and possibilities for promotion are directly related to them. Quotas help the sales manager to determine whether the salesperson's territory is either too large or too small.

The most common type of sales quota assigns a ***dollar volume of sales*** to a specific geographical area or sales territory. The sales quotas may also be related to profit quota which encourages the salesperson to sell the higher-profit items. Profits are also related to expenses, so there are expense quotas which make the salesperson more conscious of costs. Usually, the salesperson is told what her expense quotas will be, and she is often given some type of reward if her expenses are lower than expected.

Finally, there are activity quotas which are based on points rather than dollar or unit volume. Points are awarded for the number of calls made, the number of new customers gained, the number of presentations made, the degree of improvement, the number of point-of-purchase items installed, and other similar accomplishments. Activity quotas serve to motivate the salesperson, and she is usually rewarded for her accomplishments in money or prizes.

In setting sales quotas in dollars, the sales manager will first study the sales potential in each area or territory. If the "sales force summary" method is used, she automatically has the estimates for each geographic unit. However, if the "management consensus" method is used, she has a total figure which must be broken down and assigned to the respective areas or territories. In order to do this, she must have a market index, and one of the most widely used indexes of this sort is the Sales Management's annual "Survey of Buying Power."

In many instances, the forecast for a particular area or territory will automatically become the quota. For example, of a 100 percent dollar volume expected for a given territory, which three salespeople are assigned to cover, salesperson A might be given a quota of 45 percent; salesperson B, 30 percent; and salesperson C, 25 percent. However, adjustments are sometimes necessary, and the sales manager may assign quotas of 50 percent, 35 percent, and 30 percent respectively for salespeople A, B, and C making a total of 115 percent. Such a quota is an "incentive quota" and is designed to both motivate and to insure that the original quota of 100 percent will be made. On the other hand, the quotas may be lowered because the sales manager knows that the salespeople involved are too inexperienced to achieve a combined quota of 100 percent. In such a case, she might therefore set the quota at 90 percent for the territory and offer a bonus to those salespeople who achieve in excess of their respective quotas.

It should be noted that quotas should be practical and realistic. If they are too high or too low, they will usually fail to accomplish their objectives. They should also be understood and accepted by those who will be involved in achieving the quotas. Many sales managers encourage the participation of the salespeople in setting up quotas because it makes them better informed and more responsive. Quotas should also be fair and accurate and based on territorial potential rather than the sales manager's hunches or prejudices. Finally, there must be continuous follow-through on quotas, and the annual figure should be analyzed and reviewed each month.

 **Indicate whether each of the following statements is true or false**

1. Sales quotas are very important in selling, for without them there can be no effective planning and control.
2. Dollar volume quotas are the only kind used by most sales forces.
3. In many instances, the forecast for a particular area or territory will automatically become the quota.
4. Quotas set very high will usually motivate salespeople to work harder and will result in effective sales stimulation.

Answer

1. True. Sales quotas are applied to salespeople, territories, product lines, buyers, and periods of time to help the manager plan and control sales compensation, allocation of effort, and other sales functions.
2. False. Dollar volume quotas are the most common, but most sales forces also use margin and profit quotas, expense quotas, and activity quotas to get more control over these areas.
3. True. Although the forecast may become the quota, adjustments are often necessary because of the expertise and experience of salespeople, geographical differences, and other territory variables.
4. False. Quotas should be practical and realistic. Very high or very low quotas usually fail to accomplish their objectives.

Salespeople's compensation plan

Another important responsibility of the sales manager is to decide how the salespeople should be compensated. Basically, she wants to introduce a plan for compensating salespeople that will attract them in the first place, keep them in the company fold, and be sufficiently generous to motivate them to improve performance. At the same time, the plan must keep costs at a satisfactory level. Sales managers recognize that there are differences among salespeople, territories, products, and buyers. Accordingly, they want a plan that is flexible enough to apply to varying conditions. The plan adopted must also be in harmony with plans that are used for paying other company employees.

Salespeople, on the other hand, want a compensation plan which will give them a satisfactory income. Generally, they want two types of income: a steady income to cover basic living expenses and an added compensation which serves as an incentive and rewards them for certain levels of achievement. They also want a plan which is geared to those factors which they can control. This is sometimes difficult to achieve because market conditions may have changed and the plan under which the salespeople are paid is no longer appropriate. In addition, salespeople want a plan which is fair, which makes prompt payments, and one which is easy to understand and compute.

There are three basic compensation plans: (1) straight salary, (2) straight incentive, and (3) salary plus incentive. Under the straight salary plan, the salesperson is paid a fixed amount on a weekly or monthly basis. The advantages of this plan to the sales manager are that it gives her more direct control over the work of the salespeople. It is clear, specific, and relatively easy to administer. Payment on a regular and continuing basis gives the salespeople security and stability. It is also very appropriate for paying new employees or when introducing new products. Arguments against this plan are that it provides little incentive, and a greater burden is thrown on the sales manager for motivating the salespeople and supervising their work. Also, this plan sometimes is unfair--particularly when it rewards older and less efficient salespeople more than they deserve in comparison with the younger and more aggressive salespeople or vice versa. The plan must also be reviewed frequently, for it can quickly become out of date.

Under the straight commission plan, the salesperson is paid according to her performance or the amount she sells. The commission rate can either be fixed or paid on a sliding scale. Its principal merits are that is provides incentive and rewards the salesperson in proportion to her efforts. The commission salesperson also enjoys greater freedom in performing her work, and this plan generally attracts more capable salespeople. Its disadvantages are that the sales manager has less control over the salesperson's activities. It is sometimes difficult to establish commission rates which are fair in all cases, and earnings of the salesperson can fluctuate greatly, thereby giving her a feeling of insecurity and sometimes encouraging her to resort to high-pressure selling. Other problems are that house accounts (those accounts handled by the company rather than a salesperson) can cause resentment, and it is often difficult to divide a commission, which is earned by two salespeople.

The salary-plus-commission plan is a compromise pattern, which attempts to secure the advantages of both the straight salary and straight commission plans. Studies indicate that approximately 60 percent of the sales managers use this plan. There are four basic types of combination plans: (1) salary plus commission, (2) drawing account plus commission, (3) salary plus bonus, and (4) the point system.

Salary plus commission is the most common of the combination plans and is appropriate for salespeople who have to service the products they sell. Salaries under this plan can vary from 20 to 90 percent of the salesperson's total earnings. Sometimes the salary figure is geared to the cost of living, and the commission is based on sales. Or the commission may be geared to sales volume over a given amount for a particular period of time. This plan involves more bookkeeping and therefore can be expensive to administer.

A drawing account is a system of payment whereby the salesperson is paid in advance, and then she later repays the amount drawn from the commissions she earns. The amount is fixed, and she draws a given amount of money each week or month. Under a guaranteed draw, if the salesperson's commissions are lower than the draw, she does not have to repay the draw. Under the non-guaranteed draw, however, the salesperson is obligated to repay the amount advanced to her from future commissions. Drawing accounts tends to give the salesperson greater security, but they also involve increased administrative work.

A bonus is a sum of money given to the salesperson at the end of a given period for above average achievement or performance. One of the most common bonuses is the Christmas bonus. Because of the uncertainties involved with the bonus plan, it generally has less incentive value. However, it can be effectively used for rewarding salespeople on the basis of calls made, number of new accounts gained, increases in sales volume, degree of improvement, and other similar accomplishments.

In a company where activity quotas are set up, the point system may be used. Under this plan the sales manager rewards the salesperson with points for various types of accomplishment. Generally, the salesperson receives a given number of points for every $100 of sales volume, and the high-profit items in her line are assigned the highest points. Points may also be earned for the number of calls made, number of demonstrations, new accounts, and other similar accomplishments. Plus or credit points are the most common, but sometimes there can be negative or penalty points. If the salesperson earns 800 points for a given month and the value of each point is one dollar, she receives a salary of $800. This system is rather complicated and difficult to administer and therefore is not widely used.

Compensation plans vary greatly, with the combination patterns being the most common. Regardless of the plan chosen, the sales manager will attempt to choose one, which motivates the salespeople to maximum performance, and simultaneously one that is economical to administer.

 **Indicate whether each of the following statements is true or false**

1. Under a straight salary compensation plan, the salesperson is paid according to her performance or the amount that she sells.
2. Straight commission salary plans provide considerable incentive and reward the salesperson in proportion to her efforts.
3. The most common form of sales compensation is salary plus commission.
4. A "bonus" is merely another term for a "commission."

Answer

1. False. Under the straight salary plan, the salesperson is paid a fixed amount on a weekly or monthly basis, and payment is not based on sales.
2. True. The straight commission plan provides much incentive for the salesperson, but it is sometimes difficult to set fair commission rates, and management loses some control over the activities of the salesperson.
3. True. A salary-plus-commission system compensates the salesperson for selling and servicing customers. The terms of such a contract vary according to the company; its products, customers, and channels; and other such circumstances.
4. False. Bonuses differ from commissions in that they are not tied as directly to quantitative results. For instance, one might receive a Christmas bonus based on performance but not on a specific dollar volume.

Salespeople's expenses

In addition to obtaining effective selling performance, the sales manager must control salespeople's expenses if satisfactory profits are to be made. Personal selling expenses can amount to thousands of dollars each year per salesperson and generally include transportation from town to town, local transportation, meals, tips, lodging, telephone and telegraph costs, mailing costs, laundry and valet expenses, and gifts and entertainment. Policies concerning the latter items vary widely, and there are differing opinions as to the extent of entertaining and gift giving that is effective, permissible, or ethical.

Sales expenses should be handled so as not to allow expense reimbursement to become a source of income. The salesperson should be reimbursed only for the true amount of expenses she incurs. A good expense plan should also be clear, flexible, and economical to administer.

There are four basic patterns for paying expenses. The first plan is where the salesperson pays all her own expenses. For example, she may receive a total commission of 10 percent, of which 7 percent represents income or earnings, and the remaining 3 percent goes for expenses. This plan is relatively simple to administer, but it gives management little authority in controlling expenses and sometimes encourages salespeople "to skimp" on what they spend in order to increase their income. For these reasons this plan is not widely used.

A second plan for paying expenses is the unlimited reimbursement plan. Under this system there are no maximum limits, and the salesperson is simply paid for the expenses she submits. This plan gives the sales manager little control over expenses and could lead to considerable padding and abuse. For this plan to work effectively with salespeople, they must be quite conscientious and responsible. A variation of this plan is where the salesperson is required to submit an itemized report and each expense is separately examined and approved. This procedure is more time-consuming than the lump-sum version, but it gives the sales manager more control over expenses and also helps to reduce padding. This particular plan is very popular and is one of the most widely used plans for paying expenses.

A third pattern is the limited reimbursement plan. Under this system the salesperson may be limited to a maximum total for a given period, such as a total of $40 per day or $200 per week. Or the total may be broken down, with maximum totals for each type of expense, so that there would be separate maximum totals for travel, for meals, lodging, and so on. This plan is a little difficult to administer, but it can be a good one if the maximum ceilings are realistic and adequate.

The fourth plan is the flat expense allowance. Under this system the salesperson, instead of having a given percentage of her commission to cover expenses, is paid a flat dollar amount each day or week. It is a "per diem" method for handling expenses. It is clear and easy to administer. It is the sales manager's responsibility to see that the figure is no higher or lower than it should be. Sometimes the salesperson will "skimp" in order to make money on her allowance, and there is always the problem of her eliminating certain activities altogether if she has exceeded her allowance for a given period.

Regardless of the plan used, expenses seem to be always increasing, and they have an important bearing on profits. Effective control of expenses is a constant challenge to the sales manager and will greatly determine her success or failure.

Characteristics of a successful sales manager

A sales manager must possess many skills and attitudes, which will vary by company and industry. The following list indicates some of the most important ones.

- The sales manager must know how to get along and work effectively with and through other people.
- She must be skillful in the act of communication and persuasion.
- She must be able to motivate and lead others.
- She must understand others and know how to help them.
- She must know how to analyze and select new salespeople.
- She must be competent in evaluating the performance of salespeople and know how to effectively train them.
- She must know how to analyze and interpret varying types of data.
- She must know how to plan and organize.
- She must be capable of withstanding continual pressure and tension.
- She must be imaginative and creative.
- She must be flexible and capable of adapting to change.
- If she expects to achieve high standards, she must be dedicated and professionally minded.

Indicate whether each of the following statements is true or false

1. Sales expenses should be handled so as not to allow expense reimbursement to become a source of income for the salesperson.
2. When a salesperson pays all her own expenses, she cannot be prevented from "skimping" on what she actually spends in order to increase her income.
3. Sales expenses are the concern of the salespeople and not a major concern for most sales managers.
4. All sales managers need the same skills and attitudes to be successful.

Answer

1. True. Salespeople should neither make nor lose money when reimbursed for the expenses they incur. They should be reimbursed for the true amount they incur.
2. True. Letting a salesperson pay all her own expenses is an easy plan to administer, but it gives management little authority in controlling expenses and sometime results in "skimping" on sales spending.

3. False. Expenses seem to be always increasing and have a direct effect on profits. Effective control of expenses is a constant challenge to sales managers and greatly determines their success or failure.

4. False. The skills and attitudes needed by a sales manager vary by company and industry, but she should be able to work with and through others; be a skillful communicator; be able to understand and motivate others; be able to analyze, if plan, and organize; and be dedicated to her profession.

CHAPTER 18

Selection and Training of Salespeople

Effective selling begins with selecting persons who have the potential and desire to be successful salespeople and then giving them the proper training. Higher profit margins, increased competition, the high rate of turnover, and high costs of training have put more emphasis on better selection and training procedures. Present-day sales managers tend to reject the idea that "try out and fire" is a good enough basis for building a sales force. Most large companies, and even some smaller ones, now approve selecting and training of salespeople in an organized and scientific manner, using the tools provided by psychological testing and research.

Current methods used for selecting salespeople

The methods used for selecting salespeople will vary depending upon the type of product or service being sold, the size and objectives of the company, the conditions prevailing in the labor market, and the philosophies of management. The selection package, however, generally includes an application blank, an interview, the use of tests, and other selection tools such as a medical examination, personal references, and investigations by bonding companies.

The application blank normally asks for:
a) Personal data including the applicant's name, address, telephone number, sex, age height, weight, health, marital status, and size of family.
b) Education, including schools attended, addresses, dates programs majored in, and degrees received.

c)   Employment record, including name of employer, address, dates of employment, job title and duties, salary earned, and reasons for leaving.

d)   Military service, including branch of service, dates, rank, duties, special awards and citation, and type of discharge.

e)   Special activities, including name of organization, dates, offices held, awards, and hobbies.

f)   References, which usually include the names and addresses of former employers, teachers, doctors, ministers, and businesspeople. Relatives and friends are normally excluded.

Most companies use an unweighted application blank, as illustrated in Figure 18.1, which gives a comprehensive picture of the applicant. Others, however, will sometimes use a weighted application blank which assigns points to various factors having a close relationship to successful selling.

Figure 18.1: The application form

APPLICATION FOR SALES REPRESENTATIVE POSITION

1. Personal Information

Name: ____
         Last   First   Middle   Maiden

Date of Birth: DD   MM   YYYY

Marital Status: ☐ Single   ☐ Married   ☐ Widowed   ☐ Divorced

Address: ____
         Street   P.O. Box   City   Island

Email Address: ____

Telephone Contacts: Home (242) ____________   Work (242) ____________   Cell (242) ____________

Place of Birth: ____________________   **Nationality:** ____________________

Have you ever been convicted of a crime? ☐ Yes   ☐ No

If yes, please explain: ____

____

____

____

____

Number of Children: ____________   **Number of Dependants other than spouse/children:** ____________

2. Professional References

Give below the names of three/four individuals (not relatives, friends, political dignitaries or ministers of religion) who know you well and to whom the Company can refer. Please include last employer.

Name	Address	Telephone	Years Acquainted
1.			
2.			
3.			
4.			

3. General Information

Do you have any relatives in our employment? ☐ Yes ☐ No
If yes, state name, relationship and department:

Do you own a car? ☐ Yes ☐ No
If yes, what is the make and year of the car?

Have you ever sold insurance? ☐ Yes ☐ No
If yes, what type?

Have you had any other selling experience? ☐ Yes ☐ No
If yes, what did you sell?

Have you ever applied to our Company before? ☐ Yes ☐ No

If yes, which Department? ________________________ *When?* ________________

Referred by: ________________________

4. Education

Secondary School

School: ________________________ **When:** ________________

Graduate: ☐ Yes ☐ No   **Standard Attained:** ________________

Achievements: *(No. of BGCSEs and/or O'Levels)*

Subjects & Grades:

1.	2.
3.	4.
5.	6.
7.	8.
9.	10.

Post Secondary School

School: ________________________ **When:** ________________

Graduate: ☐ Yes ☐ No   **Standard Attained:** ________________

Achievements: *(Degree)*

Other Training/Designations

School/Organization: ________________________   When: ________________________

Graduate: ☐ Yes ☐ No   Standard Attained: ________________________

Achievements: ________________________

Do you plan to continue your education? ☐ Yes ☐ No

If yes, when: ________________________   *Course:* ________________________

Which foreign languages do you:

Speak:	Read:	Write:

5. Employment History

Name & Address of Employer	Job Title	MM/YY	Specific Reason for Leaving
1.			
2.			
3.			
4.			
5.			

Have you ever been terminated? ☐ Yes ☐ No

If yes, organization(s), please explain: ________________________

____

____

Have you ever worked at Family Guardian in the past? ☐ Yes ☐ No

If yes, provide: Job Title ________ Dept ________ Supervisor ________

Reason for leaving: ________________________

____

____

6. Other Activities

Are you a member of:

Rotary, Kiwanis or any other Service Club?   ☐ Yes ☐ No

Attend Regularly?   ☐ Yes ☐ No   **How Often?** _______________

Hold Office?   ☐ Yes ☐ No

Any Civic Organizations (e.g. Red Cross)?   ☐ Yes ☐ No

Attend Regularly?   ☐ Yes ☐ No   **How Often?** _______________

Hold Office?   ☐ Yes ☐ No

Any Other Organization?   ☐ Yes ☐ No

Attend Regularly?   ☐ Yes ☐ No   **How Often?** _______________

Hold Office?   ☐ Yes ☐ No

Do you have any religious customs, which may govern your work hours, dress code or other practices?   ☐ Yes ☐ No

If yes, please explain: _______________

____

____

What hobbies do you have? Please give details below of activities, hobbies and offices held.

____

____

____

____

7. Your Health

Please describe any illnesses you may have had in the past five (5) years:

____

____

Do you have any medical conditions *(including pregnancy)* **that warrants ongoing medical treatment or medication?**   ☐ Yes ☐ No

If yes, please describe: _______________

____

____

7. Your Health *Continued*

Do you have any medical conditions or impairment that might compromise your ability to
perform the duties of the position applied for?   ☐ Yes ☐ No

If yes, please describe:

In case of an emergency, please provide spouse's name and contact information:

Name:

Telephone Contacts: Work (242)   Cell (242)

I CERTIFY THAT THE ANSWERS GIVEN IN THIS APPLICATION ARE TRUE AND COMPLETE TO THE BEST OF
MY KNOWLEDGE. I AUTHORIZE INVESTIGATION OF ALL STATEMENTS CONTAINED IN THIS APPLICATION.
I UNDERSTAND THAT NEITHER THIS APPLICATION NOR ANY OFFER OF EMPLOYMENT CONSTITUTES AN
EMPLOYMENT CONTRACT UNLESS FAMILY GUARDIAN AND I EXECUTE A WRITTEN AGREEMENT TO
THAT EFFECT. I UNDERSTAND THAT ONCE HIRED, ANY MISREPRESENTATION OR OMISSION OF FACTS IN
THIS APPLICATION OR INTERVIEW(S) IS CAUSE FOR DISMISSAL. I UNDERSTAND THAT A DRUG TEST AND
PHYSICAL EXAMINATION FORM A PART OF THIS APPLICATION PROCESS*. I FURTHER UNDERSTAND
THAT IF EMPLOYED I WILL UNDERGO A 3-MONTH PROBATIONARY EMPLOYMENT PERIOD.

Signature of Applicant   Date

*** Please note:** All candidates considered for employment will be required to submit copies of BGCSE/Diploma certificates,
three written references (including former employer), a recent police certificate (issued within last 6 months) and copies of
passport information. A copy of your National Insurance card and two (2) passport photos are required once hired.
Additionally, candidates are required to complete a background release form authorizing our Company to perform a
background check, in the event that you are given a job offer. This form will be provided to your current employer after you
have accepted our job offer.

The personal interview

Basically, there are two types of personal interviews: the preliminary or screening
interview, which serves to weed out applicants who obviously are unsuited for the
job, and the secondary or follow-up interview which is designed to obtain additional
information from the applicant.

Interviews may be further distinguished as planned or structured versus non-
directive or informal. Group interviews are also used. The planned interview is very
carefully organized on the basis of specific objectives, what types of information will
be sought and given, how the interview will be conducted, and how much time will be
spent in conducting it. The non-directive interview, on the other hand, is not organized
and conducted in accordance with a list of predetermined objectives and questions.
In this type of interview, the applicant is given the responsibility for determining the

nature of the conversation. The advantages claimed for this type of interview are that the applicant is more likely to reveal her true self than she is in the planned interview, where she tends to give answers that she thinks the interviewer wants. It is also easier for the interviewee to relax. However, the non-directive interview may fail to secure answers to important questions, and sometimes the things an applicant doesn't talk about may be just as important as the items she mentions.

The depth interview is designed to obtain more complete and detailed information on specific questions. For example, a normal question to ask is what hobbies an applicant might have. In most instances, simply naming the hobby will suffice, but in the depth interview additional questions are asked such as:

- Why do you like this particular hobby?
- How did you get started in it?
- Approximately how much time and money do you spend on it? How does this hobby help you in your work?

The emphasis in the depth interview is on the "whys," and it is designed to obtain the person's reasons and feelings for doing something that might relate to her qualifications for selling.

 ## Indicate whether each of the following statements is true or false

1. The best way to increase corporate sales is to simply hire more salespeople.
2. Most companies use an unweighted application blank as part of the selection process.
3. Nondirective interviews are not organized in accordance with a list of predetermined objectives and questions.
4. Depth interviews are designed to find out such things as what hobbies the applicant might have, what other interests, and so on.

Answer

1. False. Effective selling begins with selecting persons who have the potential and desire to sell and then training them properly. Simply hiring more people will not result in greater profits in the long run.
2. True. Most companies use an unweighted application blank, but others use a weighted blank, which assigns points to various factors having a close relationship to success in selling.
3. True. The advantage of a non-directive interview is that the applicant is more likely to reveal her true self.
4. False. The emphasis in depth interviews is on the "whys," and it is designed to obtain the person's reasons and feelings for doing certain things.

The personal interview (continued)

In the group interview the applicant is interviewed by several persons at one time rather than by a single interviewer. This type of interview saves time and provides an opportunity for seeing how the applicant will respond and adapt to different types of persons. A disadvantage is that some applicants find it difficult to relax in the presence of several persons and may develop a defensive attitude, particularly if several persons are asking her questions that she thinks might be designed to trap her.

Another type of group interview is where several applicants are present at the same time, and all are interviewed by a single interviewer. Under this method, all the applicants get the same information under the same conditions. However, it is less personal, and the interviewer is unable to question each person as extensively as would be the case where each applicant is interviewed separately.

Most sales managers place considerable emphasis on the personal interview because it allows them to observe the personality traits of the candidate in a live and realistic manner. Questions frequently asked are:

- Why do you wish to pursue a career in selling?
- Why are you interested in our particular company?
- What are your major strengths and weaknesses?
- What do you want to be or become in 5, 10, 20 years from now?
- What have you done to prepare yourself for a career in selling?

When the candidate answers these questions, both what she says and how she says it are evaluated in order to determine whether she has the necessary traits to succeed in selling.

Psychological tests

Special tests are widely used today in the selection process. The ones most commonly employed are intelligence, personality, interest, and sales aptitude tests.

Intelligence tests are designed to measure mental ability. The Otis Self-Administering Test of Mental Ability is one of the most frequently used tests of this type. Generally, companies will also attempt to differentiate between abstract or mechanical intelligence versus social intelligence because of the greater applicability of the latter type of intelligence in almost all types and levels of selling.

Personality tests attempt to measure the presence of such traits as self-confidence, independence, aggressiveness, self-reliance, ambition, emotional stability, optimism, and other similar traits closely related to success in selling. There are many different types of personality tests. One of the most widely used ones is the Bernreuter Personality Inventory published by the Stanford University Press.

Interest tests are designed to measure the extent to which a person will like or dislike the various activities connected with selling. The Strong Vocational Interest Blank and Kuder Preference Record are representative of this type of test.

Finally, there are *sales aptitude* tests which are designed to determine the capacity or latent ability a person has to become a successful salesperson. Such characteristics as determination, persistence, and the desire to influence people are measured. An *achievement* test, on the other hand, measures the degree or level of competence given task or activity. In addition, there are many other specialized tests which are specifically designed for individual companies. These tests measure a person's degree of achievement in such related areas as arithmetic, bookkeeping, language ability, and so on.

In using tests in selecting applicants, it should be remembered that most testing procedures are based on averages or the "normal" type of employee. Though this information is helpful, it should not automatically eliminate persons who do not fit the stereotype and who might under certain circumstances become successful in selling. Another danger of testing is that it may eliminate highly creative people. Consequently, tests should be interpreted with great care and evaluated in relation to the other selection processes. Some tests are also very complex and may have to be administered and interpreted by a trained psychologist.

 Indicate whether each of the following statements is true or false

1. Group interviews invariably consist of several interviewers and one candidate.
2. Considerable emphasis is placed on the personal interview in the selection process.
3. The Otis Self-Administering Test of Mental Ability, the Bernreuter Scale, and The Strong Vocational Blank are all psychological tests which are used in selecting sales personnel.
4. Various selection tests may be combined to eliminate any subjective evaluation on the part of management.

Answer

1. False. Group interviews may be as described, but another group format would consist of one interviewer and several candidates.
2. True. The personal interview allows management to observe the personality traits of candidates in a live and realistic manner.
3. True. Companies generally use intelligence tests (Otis), personality tests (Bernreuter), interest tests (Strong), and a sales aptitude test in the selection process.

4. False. Though test information is helpful, it should not automatically eliminate persons who do not fit the stereotype and might be successful salespeople. Tests should be used with care and evaluated in relation to other selection processes.

Purposes of training

Training programs play a vital part in developing an effective sales force. In addition to motivating salespeople and increasing their productivity, these programs are also designed to decrease turnover, develop better morale, secure more effective control over the selling effort, improve customer relations, and help to reduce selling costs. The programs will also vary in relation to the amount of money available for training, the type of product or service being sold, and the experience of the salesperson. With new recruits, for example, an attempt will be made to achieve all of the latter objectives, whereas, with more experienced salespeople, the purpose of the program may be narrowed and aimed at introducing a new product or promotional program.

General content of training programs

Typical training program content covers:
- ***General company information*** including its history, organization, identification of executive personnel, policies, and promotion.
- ***Company operating information*** including credit policies and practices, shipping, service, handling complaints, compensation plan, quotas, and control of expenses.
- ***Product information*** including classification of customers, buying motives and habits, and special problems.
- ***Market information*** covering territory assignments, market potentials, routing procedures, general and local business conditions, and competition.
- ***Sales training*** (as opposed to product training) which relates to all phases of the sales process such as:
- Developing a selling personality.
- Methods for prospecting.
- Analyzing consumers.
- Sales approaches.
- Methods for organizing the sales presentation.
- Communication and persuasion.
- Handling objections.
- Closing.
- Building a customer following.
- Methods for evaluating and improving both selling and nonselling duties.

Personnel used in training programs

Personnel used in training salespeople generally come from three sources: company-line executives, staff trainers, and outside consultants. ***Company-line executives*** are such persons as senior salespeople, field supervisors, and sales managers. The advantages of training by these people are that they are more familiar with the actual work and problems of the salespeople, and they themselves are generally highly successful in selling. The main drawbacks of using company-line executives are that they often are too busy and lack the time for such work. In addition, these people may be highly successful in selling, but this does not guarantee that they will be effective teachers.

Staff trainers are persons who are employed to serve as trainers and also persons recruited from other departments in the company. A professional sales trainer is usually well qualified to teach and is given sufficient time to develop training programs. A staff trainer does not have the authority of a line executive, and additional costs are incurred in maintaining a separate training department. The advantages of using persons drawn from other departments is that they can provide real expertise in areas related to selling, and their participation does not add much to the cost of the training program. Again, however, these people are less familiar with actual selling, they often do not have adequate time, and they may or may not be good teachers.

Outside consultants can be obtained from firms and agencies which specialize in sales training. College professors who teach selling and sales management can also be used, as well as other recognized authorities on selling. These outside consultants are particularly appropriate for smaller and medium-sized firms which cannot afford the costs of having a full-time trainer. However, large companies also use outside consultants, since they often can do a more effective job of teaching various parts of the program. These outside consultants usually are experts in their field, are good teachers, and they have the latest information on selling and sales management. The major disadvantage of using such a person is that sometimes they are unable to relate as specifically as is desired to a particular product or service.

Methods for training

The five methods commonly used for conducting training programs are the lecture method, discussion, demonstrations, role playing, and on-the-job or field training.

Although the ***lecture*** method can cover a great deal of material over a relatively short period of time, it is not always appropriate for teaching certain areas of selling. For example, the lecture may be appropriate for telling salespeople how to secure prospects, but in teaching how to open or close the sale, other methods are generally more effective. The lecture method is also more appropriate for initial sales training programs rather than advanced or refresher courses. Consequently, it is usually more beneficial for new salespeople and of lesser value for experienced ones.

Discussion includes question and answer sessions, cases, round tables, and panels. This method has considerable flexibility involves greater participation, and is generally more interesting. As a result, it has wide acceptance and is one of the most popular methods used for training salespeople. Its main weakness is that often it cannot be used with new or green salespeople, as they do not have the knowledge or experience to conduct intelligent and profitable discussions.

The **demonstration** is especially adaptive to selling because so much of selling relates to showing or actually demonstrating the product or service. Seeing is infinitely more effective than hearing, and also increases its likelihood of being remembered. The sales presentation can also be made easier to understand by using charts, slides, films, video tape recordings, and other visual aids.

Role playing consists of creating artificial but realistic situations which will simulate actual conditions in the field. Situations in everyday selling are acted out, thereby giving the student a better understanding of and feeling for the problems she will encounter. It is an excellent and effective method for training. Its major limitation is that role playing is more involved than it appears. Consequently, it can be good or bad depending upon the skill of the leader, and the ability of the participants to act out their roles in a realistic manner.

On-the-job training is used in the final stages of the training program. It involves actual calls in the field with the sales supervisor, trainer, or a senior salesperson accompanying the new salesperson to observe what she is doing. It is a practical and effective method for training which specifically relates to live and actual problems. Its main drawback is that it is very time consuming for the observers; however, this factor is insignificant in relation to the many other benefits that can be obtained from using this method.

In summary, there are several and uniquely different methods for training salespeople. Each has its respective advantages and disadvantages and most training programs will use a combination of methods.

Mistakes to avoid

One of the greatest mistakes in training is to underestimate its importance. Some sales managers feel that formalized training is unnecessary, as they believe that actual experience is the most important teacher. It cannot be denied that there is a close relationship between experience and successful selling. However, the increased costs and competition in selling make it necessary to minimize the errors that can be made by relying solely on experience. The salesperson's work today is also more involved than it used to be and requires a higher level of education and training.

A second common error is to conduct training on a periodic or sporadic basis. It is sometimes assumed that if a person completes a training program, she will automatically remember and continue to practice what she has learned. Nothing is further from the truth; the very nature of selling requires that the salesperson be motivated and trained on a continuing basis. A professional never stops learning or attempting to improve herself. Consequently, if selling is to become more professionalized and to fulfill its several objectives, then training must be continuous.

A third common mistake in training is for management to identify the problems and determine the purposes of the program with little or no consultation with the salespeople. Such an approach encounters resistance and is almost doomed from the start, for it fails to secure the participation of the very persons for whom the program is intended. Hence, if the program is to be realistic and effective, than it certainly should include the salespeople in the initial stages of determining the objectives and content of the program.

 Indicate whether each of the following statements is true or false

1. Lien personnel such as senior salespeople are often used effectively to train new salespeople.
2. The lecture method of sales training is usually more beneficial for new salespeople than for experienced ones.
3. Role playing is a technique which tends to prevent salespeople from taking salesmanship training seriously.
4. Little formalized sales training is necessary because the best place to train salespeople is in the field.

Answer

1. True. The advantage of using field people is that they are generally successful in selling, but they are often too busy to do such training work.
2. True. The lecture method may be appropriate for telling salespeople what to do, but in explaining how to do it other methods generally are more effective.
3. False. Role-playing is a serious approach to salesmanship. It actually consists of creating artificial sales situations giving the sales student a feeling of the problems she will encounter in the field and an opportunity to practice making presentations.
4. False. The increased costs and competition in selling make it necessary to minimize the errors made in the field by inexperienced salespeople without proper training.

CHAPTER 19

The Sales Force of the Future and Social Media Marketing

What will the sales force of the year 2020 look like? Will it still consist of dependent operators who are assigned a territory or a quota? Will the high cost of competing in a global marketplace change the traditional salesperson? Although we can speculate about dramatic changes in the nature of personal selling, the traditional salesperson figure will likely remain intact for several decades. Why? Many products will still need to be sold personally by a knowledgeable, trustworthy person who is willing to resolve problems at any hour of the day.

Still, major changes in personal selling will occur, in large part due to technology. Though technology has increased selling efficiency, it has also resulted in more complex products, so that more sales calls are required per order in many industries. Also, because of the trend toward business decentralization, sales representatives now have more small or mid-sized accounts to service. Currently, virtually all companies provide laptop computers to all salespeople. Computer-based sales tracking and follow-up systems allow salespeople to track customers. This technology means that salespeople can assess customer-buying patterns, profitability, and changing needs more rapidly. Accessing this information via computer saves the salesperson time and allows customization of the sales presentation.

Sales teams will continue to gain in popularity because customers are looking to buy more than a product. They are looking for sophisticated design, sales, education, and service support. A sales team includes several individuals who possess unique expertise and can coordinate their efforts to help meet the needs of the particular prospect in every way possible. The salesperson acts as a team quarterback, ensuring that the account relationship is managed properly and that the customer has access to the proper support personnel.

Procter & Gamble is one company that has adopted the team approach. P&G has 22 sales executives who coordinate the sales effort of various P&G divisions in their assigned market areas. Each manager coordinates key account teams composed of sales executives from P&G's grocery division. As many as three key account teams may sell in each market. The marketing manager supervises a logistics team composed primarily of computer systems and distribution executives. The team works closely with retailers to develop mutually compatible electronic data and distribution systems. P&G hopes the team approach will reduce the pressure for trade promotions because the team provides greater service to resellers.

Salespeople of the future will have to adjust to new forms of competition with the increased capabilities and greater use of direct marketing. For example, salespeople must recognize that some customers will buy a product without contact with a salesperson. Product catalogs that feature everything from computers to classic automobiles are mailed directly to customers or ordered on the Internet. These often provide all the information about the product the customer needs to know. Questions can be answered through a toll-free number, an Internet comment form, or e-mail. Salespeople of the twenty-first century should either integrate direct marketing to support the selling process or offer the customer benefits not available through other marketing communications techniques.

On this very small planet, salespeople will also have to adjust to new sources of competition. Companies in Asia, South America, and Eastern Europe are introducing thousands of new products to industrialized nations every year. The salesperson of the future must know how to respond to foreign competitors and how to enter their markets. A program that integrates personal selling with other marketing communication tools will give salespeople more opportunity to act efficiently and have selling success.

New techniques for sales success

Recent technological advances have given salespeople more ways than ever to improve sales and productivity. To make technology work, however, you have to control it instead of letting it control you. Start by learning to use everyday tools (computer, fax, and e-mail) more efficiently and effectively. Once you know how to get the most out of technology, you can get more out of each workday.

> ▶ *Get a voice-mail advantage*. You can avoid time-consuming two-way phone conversations by outlining detail in voice-mail. Also, if you need the

person for whom you're leaving the message to take some actions, say so in the message, then say there's no need to call you back unless they have questions or problems.

▶ ***Improve your email habits.*** To avoid frequent interruptions to your workday, set aside specific, scheduled times during the day to answer your e-mail.

▶ ***Use social media.*** Social media is a new phenomenon that has grown at an exponential rate. ***Social media marketing*** refers to the process of gaining website traffic or attention through social media sites such as Facebook and Twitter.

▶ ***Get better acquainted with your PC or tablet.*** Take an hour or so before or after work for a week to learn all of your computers functions and how they can boost your productivity.

▶ ***Make a sound investment.*** You rely on technology every day to do your job, so it pays to spend a little more for equipment that won't let you down. Carefully assess your technology needs, then shop around for equipment that meets those needs without a lot of bells and whistles.

▶ ***Take a break.*** Overall increases in the speed of business can leave a salesperson feeling done in and turned out.

The drivers that make sales teams tick

Every sales force wants to improve its results. Any sales force wants to improve its results by 5 to 10 per cent. Good sales forces rework their strategy and sales process when confronted with circumstances such as customer consolidation, new product and market opportunities, technological innovation and aggressive competitive moves. The best sales forces establish processes that enable them to fine tune their performance even when the environment does not require it.

Sales force issues

Major sales force issues, challenges and concerns fall into two categories: alpha and beta concerns. Alpha concerns require immediate attention. They might include: "Customers are consolidating and our selling model no longer works"; "Technology is changing our product line and the way we need to sell"; "Competitors are attacking our most profitable segments", "How do we build a sales force for our new product line?"

Beta concerns are daily, familiar productivity issues: "How do we retain our best people?"; "How do we increase the skills and capabilities of our salespeople"; "How do we motivate salespeople?"; "How good is our salary and bonus plan?" The following provides a more complete list of contemporary sales force concerns.

Alpha concerns threaten the entire organization. The sales force must evolve or else perish at the hands of a more nimble competitor. Beta concerns are more insidious.

Nothing needs to be done immediately and managers are likely to say: "Let's do what we did last year – it worked then, didn't it?" However, beta concerns should never be taken lightly. They are today's oversights that will become problems tomorrow.

How do sales force executives go about addressing these challenges and concerns? The answer lies in developing a decision framework. The framework is based on identifying a set of sales force productivity drivers that reveal what changes must be made to address sales force challenges and concerns.

Productivity drivers

Sales force productivity drivers are made up of the decisions sales managers make and the processes they use which directly affect all parts of the selling organization. They fall into four categories.

1. Sales research includes the results of data collection and analysis that enable the organization to understand better customer-buying behavior and to segment, prioritize and target specific markets.

2. The sales force investment and organization category covers decisions on the appropriate size for the sales force, the best organizational structure, the best deployment of resources across products, markets and activities, and the right alignment of sales territories. These are of most interest to senior managers.

3. The people category includes selection (recruitment and promotion), training and development, coaching and supervision, defining and assessing selling competencies, motivation programs, and personnel evaluation and progression systems. Decisions about these factors strongly affect the interaction between the sales force and the customer. The person the customer sees is the result of hiring, training and the "success" atmosphere that the sales manager creates and fosters. These decisions have the greatest impact on sales success.

4. The sales systems category includes management decisions that directly affect the efficiency, effectiveness and job satisfaction of salespeople and hence affect customers indirectly. Compensation, incentives, benefits, sales force data, tools and other productivity enhancement programs are included.

How can these productivity drivers help managers resolve the problems of a sales force? A large global paper and packaging company provides a good illustration. The retention of its best salespeople was a major concern because personnel turnover rates in some of the divisions were as high as 40 percent a year.

Studying the sales force productivity drivers gave managers several hypotheses:

- The company was hiring people with the wrong profile.
- Training was not appropriate.
- Salespeople were not bonding with the company because the sales manager was not providing sufficient coaching and recognition.
- The compensation program was underpaying compared with the market place.
- Sales territories were not aligned to provide equal opportunity for everyone
- The company did not provide the tools to reduce tedious administrative work and identify high opportunity prospects.

Any one or all of these could help solve the turnover problem.

In another example, a pharmaceutical company was faced with launching several new products within a year. The company also wanted to protect its strong existing products. It turned to the sales force productivity drivers to establish options for developing its sales force strategy.

Results suggested several options for addressing the dual problems. The company could increase its sales force size to support its dual objectives. It could restructure parts of its sales force to create one or more specialty teams to gain access to "hard-to-see" physicians. It could identify the early adopters and influencers to help salespeople deploy their time in the most effective way during the launch. It could develop an incentive program to create both excitement for the new products and a commitment to attaining established sales goals for the existing product portfolio.

Challenges and concerns arise regularly for every sales force. Returning to the categories of alpha and beta concerns, different change processes should be used to tackle each kind of concern. The immediacy of alpha issues often requires surgery while persistent beta issues call for a good exercise routine.

The alpha change process

The alpha changes process contains three steps.

Step 1. Identify the drivers

Study the sales force productivity drivers to determine which are the salient drives. The most pressing need for the pharmaceutical company in the above example is to resize and restructure its sales force. It will lose millions if the launches are not successful or if it fails to support the existing brands.

Step 2. Identify best practices

Investigate best practices and best processes for addressing the sales force productivity driver identified in Step 1. There are various ways of determining best practices. The sales force represents a large investment for many companies. Consequently, many companies try to determine the most effective way to manage their sales forces and they frequently share their successes with non-competing companies in other industries. Benchmarking current practices across industries is one method for identifying best practices.

Consulting firms are another source for best practice insights. Some conduct hundreds of sales force studies every year covering a wide range of issues and so have a good grasp of the most effective practices.

Step 3. Implementation

Decide on the sales force driver changes and implement them quickly – successful sales forces are quick sales forces.

Companies need to be careful not simply to select those drivers that pose no threat. The most commonly selected drivers are training and compensation. They are sage. More training or a better bonus plan threatens no one. More often than not, other productivity drivers need to be addressed before considering training and compensation. How easily does a selling organization come to the realization that its main problem is an ineffective first-line sales management team?

The beta change process

It can be difficult to generate enthusiasm for the pursuit of greater productivity when a company is consistently achieving its sales target. Yet improving even some productivity drivers can increase sales by 5 to 10 per cent. For many companies, the impact will be significantly greater. The beta change process is a productivity hunt. It has three steps.

Step 1. Assess and prioritize

Beta concerns must first be diagnosed, measured and prioritized. The sales force productivity drivers need to be evaluated periodically. Two measures of these productivity drivers have proven to be useful: competency and impact. First, each decision or process is evaluated in terms of how good or how competent the selling organization is at the decision or process. Second, each decision or process is evaluated in terms of the impact the decision or process has on the selling organization's ability to succeed.

An assessment and prioritization grid can be developed with performance and importance rated on the axes from high to low. Each driver should be analyzed with regard to its position on the grid. This provides a valuable tool to assess the status of the sales force productivity drivers.

- Drivers in the "low importance, high performance" quadrant can be maintained at current levels for the time being.
- Drivers in the "high importance, high performance" quadrant need to be monitored closely to ensure their performance stays high.
- Those that fall in the "low importance, low performance" category can be monitored in case the importance of the driver increases over time.
- Top priority goes to productivity drivers with low performance and high importance for sales force success. These areas present the greatest opportunity for productivity gains.

The matrix requires measurement of both the impact and the current competency of relevant sales force productivity drivers. Method for this type of measurement have been scrutinized and continue to improve as more selling organizations adopt this approach.

Both quantitative and qualitative measures have been used to assess competency and impact. There are many quantitative measures, but territory level analysis has proven to be useful for many of the sales productivity drivers.

- If salespeople do not allocate their time effectively, they need to improve their targeting.
- If high performers are underpaid and low performers are overpaid, the compensation scheme will need to be revisited.
- If some sales territories have significant workload and others do not have enough work to keep the salesperson busy, the sales territories need re-balancing.

Consider the example of the distribution of salespeople for a cosmetics company. The workload, expressed in hours of face-to-face time required to cover all of the accounts in each territory, was calculated for each person. The results showed that the workload ranged from 375 to 1,980 hours across the total sales force of 205 people. The ideal workload had already been estimated at 1,000 hours a year for each salesperson. Allowing a 15 per cent variation either way, anyone having more than 1,150 hours or workload could not adequately cover all accounts in the territory. Anyone with fewer than 850 hours of workload had too little to do.

The company was not using its resources appropriately because 65 territories were too large and 55 were too small. This misalignment would cost the company millions each year.

Step 2. Action plan

Improvements in the sales force productivity drivers fall into two categories: "quick win" opportunities and long-term initiatives. Realigning the sales territories for the cosmetics company above is an example of a "quick-win" initiative. Longer-term initiatives might include developing a retention plan for the paper and packaging company that would include recruiting, sales manager selection, a sales assistant program to relieve the administrative burden, and an enhanced recognition program. Any action plan must balance short-term wins and long-term initiatives. The plan needs a statement of objectives, specific action items, anticipated results and a timeline.

Step 3. Implement and track

The action plan needs to be implemented and the results tracked. This year's results serve as input into the next year's assessment and sales force driver prioritization.

Current practice

Companies have used the alpha process for years. It is a necessary process for dealing with urgent needs. Implementation of the beta process is more limited but increasing. A needs assessment and prioritization every two years seems most appropriate.

Social media marketing

Social media includes the various online technology tools that enable people to communicate easily via the internet to share information and resources. It can include text, audio, video, images, podcasts, and other multimedia communications. Social media is user generated content, meaning its authors rule in the development and form for which it takes place in (channel). Its sheer development is quite remarkable, in that it is manipulated and strategically developed by the user, and its venue is a user made decision.

Social media is a new phenomenon that has grown at an exponential rate and is being used as an alternative marketing tool (see Figure 1). **Social media marketing** generally refers to using the many online services for relationship selling. Social media networks or services make innovative use of new online technologies to accomplish familiar communication and marketing goals. Some were created with consumers in mind but came to be used by thousands of businesses (such as Facebook and Twitter), while others were created specifically with business users in mind (LinkedIn is the largest of these). In addition, business professionals use a variety of specialized social networks, including those that help business owners get support and advice, those that connect entrepreneurs with investors, and those such as Segway Social and Specialized created by individual companies to enhance the sense of community among their customer bases. Some companies have created private social networks for internal use only. For example, the defense contractor Lockheed Martin created its Unity network, complete with a variety of social media applications, to meet the expectations of younger employees accustomed to social media use and to capture the expert knowledge of older employees nearing retirement.

Figure 19.1:What alternative marketing or media channels are you evaluating?*

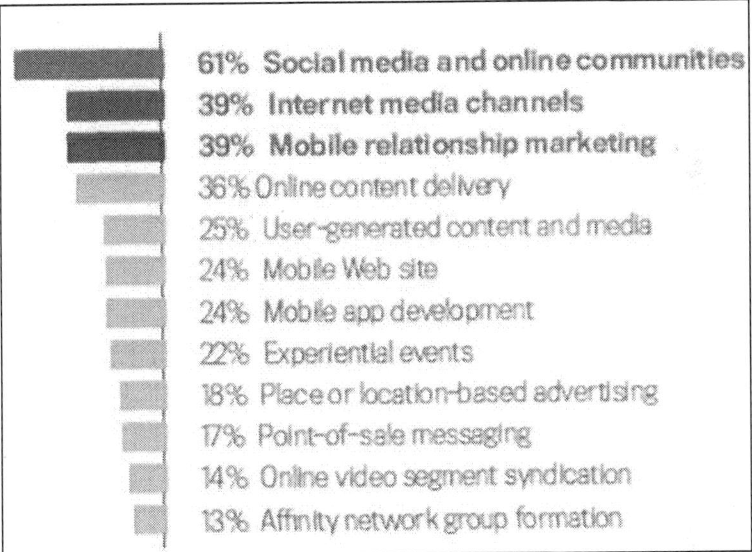

* More than 600 marketing executives' survey participants selected all options that applied.

*Source: CMO Council, **The 2011 State of Marketing.***

Blogs, Podcasts, and Vlogs are a much simpler use of social media, and much better suited for small business. The young company, or the start-up has much to benefit from these channels. These are simple to maintain, and its content allows a business (particularly smaller businesses) to detail in greater length their story. They are cheap, simple methods of stirring up a base of followers. When the followers of these social media channels engage and follow blogs, podcasts, or video logs, they are more likely to grow with that company. If consumers feel as though they are the beginning of something, they are more inclined to spread its word, and become a volunteer marketing campaign.

The Benefits

Social media marketing carries many benefits. The single most important is that you do not have to front any cash for most of these services. When weighing in on the benefits, think about whether the benefit is one that is applicable to your needs. How important is it to your business? How much time are you willing to allocate for it? What kind of a payoff would you expect?

A large audience

Hundreds of millions of users are actively engaging in social media services. This means that an ultimate benefit is how grand the audience of social media is. As of April 2012, websites like Facebook has over 900 million users worldwide. Up until that point Google was the king. Twiiter which has over 200 million users claims that millions of tweets or short messages are sent out and read everyday by followers. Businesses, celebrities, and average people such as you and me are using services similar to these on a daily basis. The audience is so large that the net that is cast out to users by business to possibly influence a user to either buy into a brand's product is large. Though not every user of a particular social media service may become a customer, the amount of people who are led into a brand is tremendous.

Branding

An integral part to a brand's marketing is its presence or the magnitude of awareness by consumers. Branding attempt to increase the visibility, awareness, or name recognition a brand has. Social media services are a great way to increase the presence of a brand with less money than traditional advertising such as television, magazines, radio, or print. With social media you can target many large segments in a more cost-effective manner than ever before. Selecting the desired people to branch out to will increase the success of social media on such a massive audience.

Relationship building

Businesses have always succeeded when establishing positive relationships with its customers or other businesses. The trust and perception of a business is directly associated to this relationship. Having a strong and secure relationship will lead to a positive brand perception. This relationship is important, and occurs over a lengthy period of time. Relationships are not built overnight, and the same is true with social media relationships. To successfully build and maintain these relationships, the following techniques are essential:

- Communicate your brand expertise in a fun and responsible manner

- ▶ Actively engage your audience and participate regularly in communication with your audience
- ▶ Add value to your brand with easy tools such as research, studies, or links to other sources of unbiased information
- ▶ Always avoid over-selling the brand, as customers are savvy and the last thing they want is an over the top sales pitch, or excessive promotion

These relationship-building techniques will grow the relationship of a brand and user and secure a strong foundation for time to come. These social relationships can lead to increased sales, positive brand perception, and at the very least a higher awareness of the brand.

The business process

Businesses are all very different. But, many businesses operate successfully by providing support to customers and collecting feedback. Social media makes it very easy to offer support for a product to a large group of people. If there is an issue, then there is a high probability that many others are facing the same issue. Social media allows a business to offer the necessary support via social media, rather than call centers or e-mail support, which to many consumers is a daunting and sometimes negative experience. Feedback is just as important in business as anything else. Feedback is an easy way to monitor a company's success or weaknesses. Social media allows users to easily offer feedback on a brand and share that with many others. Companies can leverage this information to help with research and design, product improvements, and to generally obtain an idea for what is working and what's not.

Since humans naturally gravitate at the opportunity to have their voice be heard, social media is a unique and appropriate method for consumers to air praises but in many cases complaints. Business can promptly handle unhappy customers and direct complaints to the appropriate authority to solve issues. These efforts can help to eliminate many of the "bad" experiences a customer may have had.

The negatives

Though it is evident that there are numerous advantages to using social media for growing your business there are some drawbacks to be aware of. Most services require a significant investment of time to initiate and maintain a social media marketing campaign. Simply launching a marketing campaign is not enough to obtain the full scope of benefits that social media has to offer. Maintaining and active participation and full immersion into a social media campaign are necessary for success. An increasing number of marketing departments see an upsurge in online advertising dollars through social media (see Figure 2).

Also note that social media is far reaching and rapidly moving. Thus when something negative or detrimental is conveyed across social channels, its effects can be hazardous. Social media is like a window into a personal space such as a home, and although it can be great, negative content can leak or be spread across the internet.

Figure 19.2: Investing in social media. Where will marketing departments invest their online dollars?

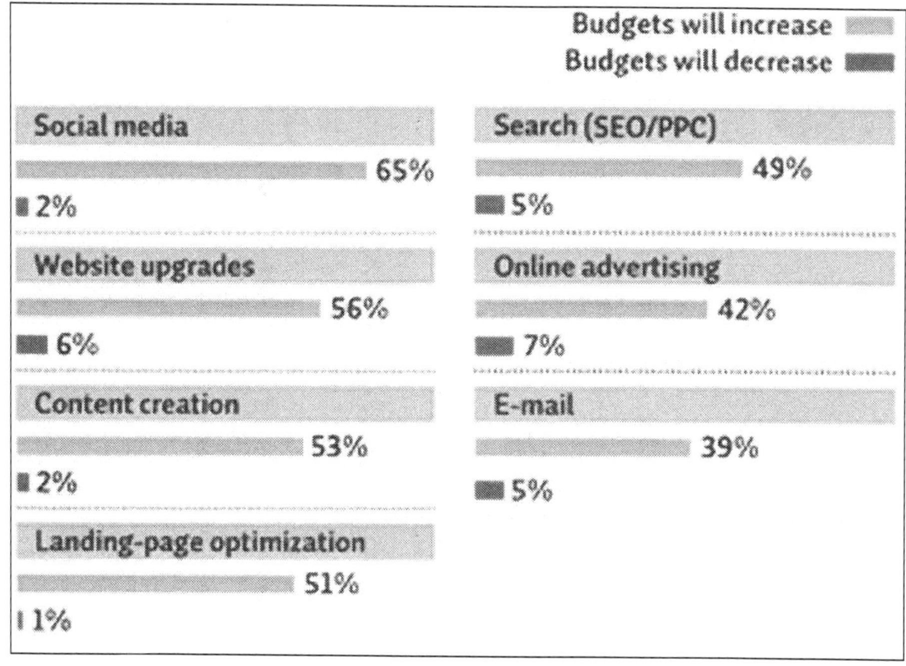

Source: 2011 Marketing Sherpa Social Marketing Benchmark Survey

Choosing the right strategy

With so many forms of social media at your disposal, strategic thought and analysis must go into which form of social media is best for the business. Social media marketing can be combined so as to not separate the two. They are not two different worlds, in fact, all the rules that apply to a traditional marketing mix are the same rules that apply to your social media marketing mix.

When deciding on what type of strategy to employ for your social media marketing mix, one of the most important and fundamental tasks is to do your research. It is wise to gain a good understanding of what segments or demographics that a social media network reaches. Who uses their services. Are they geared toward younger people? Is it predominantly men or women? Economic status? For example, when deciding what time to buy a television advertising spot, a company would first like to know that the people viewing at the time slot are potential customers. You probably would not want to advertise handbags at a department store during a football game. The same is true for spreading content across social media. However, in the case of social media these decisions can be even tougher. The reason is that the people who use such services tend to be very dispersed across different age groups, genders, incomes, and lifestyles. They are such diverse groups, but, with careful analysis, you can make the most out of your social media marketing mix by aligning the audience with your targeted segments. Every channel has its separate demographics. For example, LinkedIn is a social network consisting of predominantly professional adults.

Note that engaging in social media contact is not an easy one step process that will take care of itself. Yes, a huge advantage is that the fees are minimal. The resources that are needed are time and energy. If there is a lack of time or energy to stay with the initial commitment, then social media is probably not a strategy your business should employ. You will need to continually maintain and update your social media site or service. Also your audience will not grow that large without time. You have to be patient with your audience, and understand how social media works. Social media grows by its users. The people who view your page or follow you are the magic who spread your business name. Thus, it takes time, but to ensure that this growth is exponential, constantly have something to offer via social media. Earlier in this chapter, various tools were offered, such as offering product information or including links to unbiased research, to show your customers that you have a worthy product.

Figure 19.3 presents top goals cited by companies regarding their social media strategies.

Figure 19.3: Social media priorities

Priority	%
Communicating with customers	74%
Responding to customer questions	65%
Promoting events	60%
Generating sales leads	52%
Selling products/services	50%
Soliciting customer reviews	48%
Capturing customer data	46%
Brand monitoring	46%
Customer research	43%
Recruiting employees	43%
Employee-to-employee interactions	41%
Soliciting customer ideas	40%
Providing support	40%
Expert insights/thought leadership	38%
Training/education	37%
Customer-to-customer interactions	35%
Vendor or partner communications	27%

Source: IBM Survey of 351 Social Media Executives (www.freshnetworks.com/blog/2011/10/68-of-global-cmos-underprepared-to-manage-social-media)

Measuring success

Social media is an extension of social behavior, and social discourse is hugely important in business. That means the ROI is the highest in the world. Unfortunately, ROI numbers and other data are mostly not available. Companies must rely on other criteria to ensure they are achieving the most out of their social media marketing mix. Here are some metrics to be looked at (see Figure 19.4).

Figure 19.4: How to measure success? Most common methods by which companies measure social media marketing effectiveness.

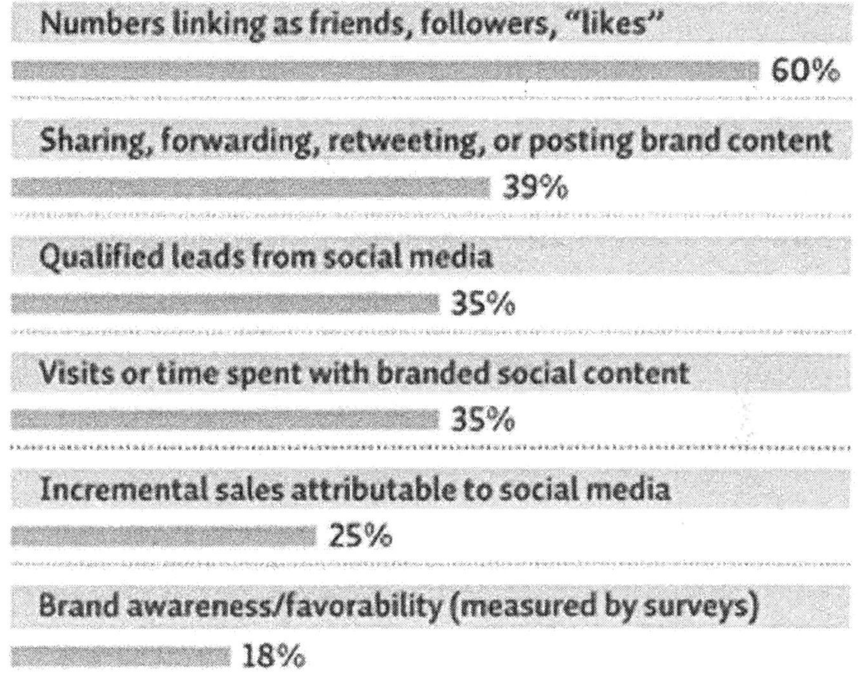

*Source: Chief Marketers, **2011 Social Marketing Survey**, October 2011*

Analytics are a great source of information

Google Analytics is an easy and very helpful measurement. Also, there are paid statistical packages for many different needs, which break down your success in social media. Although the information comes at a cost, it is quite valuable if used properly. Web metrics and advertising metrics are also available and can supplement these other measurement tools.

Here are some of the ways to measure the success of your social media marketing mix.

- ▶ ***Traffic***: You need to know the number and demographics of visitors to any website you in your marketing mix
- ▶ ***Leads:*** How many sales are made as a result of social media? This is more strategic tool for Business-2-Business (B2B) sales and high-ticket items.
- ▶ ***Search Engine Optimization:*** Many social media sites only strengthen your name in terms of searching. How can you optimize your website via search engines?

▶ **Numbers:** Evaluate your costs, sales, and profits. Trace which sales arrive from which sources to ensure that social media outlet is a viable component of your marketing mix.

Glossary

Absolute ethics Ethics, which are constant and always apply regardless of the circumstances that, might prevail.

Achievement test Test which measures the degree or level of competence a person has already achieved with regard to a given task or activity.

Acquired want A want that is learned and which also is a further refinement of a basic want.

Activity quota A quota, which is based on points, assigned to various selling activities rather than dollar or unit volume.

Advertising discount A discount in the form of an advertising allowance based on the amount and type of merchandise bought.

Analogy An example or illustration which relates one situation or circumstance with another.

Antimerger Act An act passed in 1950 and designed to prevent the lessening of competition by making it more difficult for large companies to acquire other large or even medium sized companies in their own or closely related markets.

"Appeal response" theory A theory, which states that the buyer makes a number of separate decisions in response to the appeals or stimuli, presented by the salesperson.

Aptitude test A test designed to determine the capacity or latent ability a person has to accomplish a given task.

Attitude A person's state of mind, feeling, or disposition toward something.

Automobile Information Disclosure Act An act passed in 1958 requiring the posting of the suggested retail price, the specific prices of extra equipment and options, and transportation charges on all new passenger vehicles.

Basic want A wants which is common to all human beings.

Basing point price A price determined from a given location or base point.

Benefit proof technique A technique used by the salesperson where any benefit she mentions in connection with her product or service is always followed or supported with a specific proof.

Bonus A lump sum of money given to the salesperson at the end of a given period for performance which was above average or beyond a predetermined goal.

"Buying decisions" theory A theory, which states that the buyer makes a number of separate decisions in response to the appeals or stimuli, presented by the salesperson.

Cash discount A discount which is designed to encourage and reward early or prompt payment.

C.I.F. price An abbreviation meaning "cost, insurance, and freight" which is used in export selling.

Clayton Act An act passed in 1914, which broadened the latitude of the Sherman Antitrust Act.

C.l. discount A discount given to a buyer for having bought a full "carload lot."

Close The culminating stage of the sales process in which the prospect decides whether or not she will buy the product or service.

"Cold turkey" or "cold canvas" selling A method of prospecting where the salesperson does not select prospects in accordance with a predetermined criterion.

Convenience good A product which is frequently consumed on a daily or weekly basis, is available in many stores which are located near the consumer, is competitively priced, and is generally intensively advertised. Such products as cigarettes, gasoline, or toothpaste are examples of a convenience good.

Coupon offers Certificates for a specified amount off a product.

Credit Permission to buy a product immediately and pay for it later.

Customer reference prospecting A method of prospecting in which the salesperson attempts to obtain the names of additional prospects from persons she has interviewed or customers who have purchased from her.

Daily plan An outline and schedule of the things a salesperson plans to accomplish on a given day.

Depth Interview A very complete type of interview which seeks "in depth" answers to questions.

Derived demand A demand for a particular material or commodity, which is dependent upon its end market use by the ultimate consumer.

Dyadic interaction An integrated analysis of the roles played by both parties in a sale. It is an analysis where two separate units are treated as one.

Early order discount A discount designed to encourage the buyer to order early in the season.

Emotional motive A motive based on feelings, which also is highly impulsive and not carefully planned in advance.

Ethics Practices or principles for achieving ideal behavior or character.

Fair trade price A price established by contract between a manufacturer of a branded product and a wholesaler or retailer. The manufacturer decides what the minimum price will be and the wholesaler or retailer may not sell below this established price.

F.a.s. price An abbreviation meaning, "free alongside." The seller agrees to pay the transportation charges for getting the goods within reach of the loading cranes, and at this point title passes to the buyer.

Federal Trade Commission Act An act passed in 1914 which established the Federal Trade Commission, giving it the power to investigate and to issue cease and desist orders in cases involving unfair methods of competition.

Flat expense allowance Under this system the salesperson, instead of having a given percent of her commission to cover expenses, is paid a flat dollar amount each day or week.

F.o.b. price "Free on board" a railroad car, a ship, a plane, or a motor truck. Under this price the seller assumes the transportation charges to a given shipping point, and the buyer incurs the costs beyond that point.

Fur Products Labeling Act An act passed in 1951 which requires information on the label indicating whether the fur is new or used, from what specific part of the animal it was obtained, and whether the fur is bleached or dyed.

Group discount A discount given to a group of buyers who pool or combine their purchases into a single order.

Guaranteed draw An advance payment of money to the salesperson, which does not have to be repaid, if the salesperson's commissions for the period are less than the draw.

Guaranteed price A price, which protects the buyer from any further price decreases that might occur prior to the time, the product is either used or resold to the ultimate consumer.

Hazardous Substances Labeling Act An act passed in 1960 which requires warning labels on household products containing toxic, corrosive, or flammable substances.

IMC (Integrated Marketing Communication) mix Various combinations of elements in a promotional plan: advertising, sales promotion, personal selling, public relations.

Intelligence test A test designed to measure a person's mental ability.

Interest test A test designed to measure the extent to which a person will like or dislike the various activities connected with a given type of work.

Internet marketing A form of direct marketing; also called ***online marketing***. It requires that both the retailer and the consumer have the computer and modem.

Law of effect A law related to learning, which refers to repetition of a satisfactory response.

Law of exercise A law related to learning, which refers to a form of conditioning, which elicits a second identical response to a specific stimulus, if the first response has been rewarding or satisfying to the person.

Law of readiness A law related to learning, which refers to a person's ability and willingness to solve a problem.

L.c.l. An abbreviation meaning "less than car load lot."

Learning Any change in a person's response or behavior.

List price A quoted or published price from which buyers are normally allowed discounts.

"Marketing concept" A philosophy for doing business which emphasizes two basic objectives: consumer satisfaction and profitable sales.

"Mental states" theory A theory, which maintains that the buyer's mind, passes through successive stages during the buying process. These stages: are "attention, interest, desire, action, and satisfaction."

Merchandise approach An opening or greeting in which the salesperson refers to a selling point related to the product, which the prospect is examining or handling.

Metaphor A word or phrase which refers to an object or idea in place of another by way of suggesting a comparative likeness.

Miler Tydings Act An act passed in 1937, which recognized that, all dealers in a fair trade state had to agree to price maintenance as long as one dealer had entered into such an agreement.

Mixed car lot A discount allowing the buyer to buy in smaller quantities rather than full car or truck lots of one product. Under this system, the buyer receives a balanced assortment of products and still receives a car load price.

Motivation The study of the drives, urges, desires, or wishes which influence a person to buy a particular product or service.

Negative motive A motive based on negative associations, which emphasizes the problems or dangers a person will avoid by using a particular product or service.

Net price The final price after all discounts and allowances have been deducted.

Non guaranteed draw An advance payment of money to the salesperson, which has to be repaid if the salesperson's commissions for the period are less than the draw.

Patronage motive Those considerations which cause a person to choose a particular dealer or retailer over another.

Perception The process of becoming aware of something through the senses of seeing, hearing, touching, tasting, smelling, and internal sensing.

Personality test A test which attempts to measure the degree to which a person possesses certain traits such as self confidence, aggressiveness, enthusiasm, and so on.

Persuasion The art of being able to change someone's thinking about something and also getting her to act on it.

Point system A variation of the salary plus commission method for compensating salespeople. Under this system the salesperson is rewarded with points for various types of accomplishments.

Positive motive A motive based on positive associations or benefits, which the consumer will receive from using the product or service.

Postage stamp delivered price Pricing method used when a company wishes to sell its product or service at the same price throughout its entire market.

Primary motive Those particular factors, which motivate a person to choose one general type of product or service over another.

"Problem solution" theory A theory which states that the wants, needs, or problems of the buyer serve as the salesperson's frame of reference, and she gears her presentation to showing how her product or service will fulfill these wants or solve these problems.

Program presentation A presentation, which is organized and prepared on the basis of a careful survey of the buyer's needs.

Prospecting Methods used by a salesperson to find new customers.

Pure Food and Drug Act An act passed in 1906 regulating the production, processing, and distribution of foods and drugs sold in interstate commerce.

Quantity discount A discount for buying in large quantities.

Rational motive A motive based on objective analysis and careful reasoning.

Rebates A refund of a fixed amount for a certain amount of time.

Reciprocity A practice of buying from those who buy from you.

Reinforcement A learning condition which increases the probability of an identical response, or a rewarding or satisfying situation which helps to stimulate the occurrence of the same response.

Relative ethics Ethics which are flexible and adaptable to varying circumstances.

Resale price maintenance laws Laws, which make it illegal for the manufacturer to, set or control the price at which her product will be sold in the retail market.

Retailing All activities required to market consumer goods and services to ultimate consumers.

Right mental attitude An attitude, which emphasizes the positive aspects of a situation rather than its negative points.

Robinson Patman Act An act passed in 1936 to protect small businesses by regulating price discrimination on products bought by retailers.

Role playing Using artificial but realistic situations to simulate actual conditions.

Sales force summary A forecast arrived at by estimates received from the salespeople and other sales executives.

Sales forecast An estimate of the sales that will be made for a particular period of time such as a season or year.

Sales promotion Temporary special offers intended to provide a direct stimulus to produce a desired response by customers.

Sales quota Dollar amounts that a salesperson is expected to sell in a given territory for a given period of time.

Sales spotters Persons used for prospecting who receive cash or premium rewards from the salesperson if the lead they provided her results in a sale.

Selective motive Those factors causing a person to choose one brand name over another in the same product class.

Sherman Antitrust Act Act passed in 1890 for the purpose of preventing monopolies and restraint of trade.

Shopping good A product which is infrequently consumed in comparison with a convenience good, is available in fewer outlets which are generally located farther away from the consumer. Greater variances exist in price and quality, it has a higher unit value, and there is usually considerable planning by the consumer before he purchases such a product. Examples of shopping goods are a suit, a sport jacket, an appliance, furniture, and an automobile.

Showmanship Methods used by the salesperson to emphasize and dramatize selling points.

Simile A comparison between two objects or ideas by using the words "like" or "as."

Social media (networks) Various online technology tools that enable people to communicate easily via the internet to share information and resources.

Social media marketing The process of gaining website traffic or attention through social media sites such as Facebook and Twitter.

Specialty good A product which has very special and unique characteristics. The consumer generally will "go out of her way" to purchase such a product and usually is reluctant to accept substitutes.

State fair trade laws Laws aimed at excessive price cutting of trademarked or branded merchandise and making it illegal for the manufacturer to set or control the price at which her product will be sold in the retail market.

Substitution selling An attempt by the salesperson to sell merchandises other than the specific type requested by the customer.

Suggestion selling An attempt by the salesperson to sell additional merchandise after the prospect has already made a purchase.

Tariff Act An act passed in 1930 which stipulates that the country of origin must be clearly indicated on imported articles or on their containers.

Testimonial prospecting A method of prospecting where the salesperson uses the names of well known and/or influential people to help her in selling to others.

Trade or functional discount A discount granted by the seller on the basis of the buyer's trade classification and the functions or services he performs.

"Trading up" An attempt by the salesperson to get the prospect to buy the more expensive or better quality merchandise.

Truth In Lending Act An act passed in 1968 which requires that credit terms be stated in a standard and meaningful way allowing the buyer to make comparisons.

Unfair trade practice laws Laws varying from state to state, but generally prohibiting price cutting below a specified level, which usually is set at approximately 6 percent above the invoice price.

User's expectation forecast A forecast arrived at by asking consumers or customers what and how much they plan to buy for a given period.

Vertical marketing system (VMS) A system under which a member of the distribution channel assumes a leadership role and attempts to coordinate the efforts of the channel.

Visualization The process of picturing how something will look without actually seeing it.

Wheeler Lea Act An act passed in 1938, which prevents retailers from engaging in deceptive acts or practices in pricing.

Wool Products Labeling Act An act passed in 1939, which requires that the specific type and percentage amount of wool, plus other fibers or fillers, be indicated on the label.

Zone price An equalized price for a product sold in different zones or geographical areas.

Index